Walks around Akron

Rediscovering a City in Transition

RUSS MUSARRA &
CHUCK AYERS

THE UNIVERSITY OF AKRON PRESS

The publication of this book was made possible through the generous support
of the Summit County Historical Society.

Articles and the accompanying images dated 1987–2000 are reprinted with
the permission of the *Akron Beacon Journal*.

LIBRARY OF CONGRESS CATALOGING-IN-PUBLICATION DATA
Musarra, Russ.
Walks around Akron : rediscovering a city in transition /
Russ Musarra and Chuck Ayers. — 1st ed.
p. cm. — (Series on Ohio history and culture)
Includes index.
ISBN 978-1-931968-42-3 (cloth : alk. paper) —
ISBN 978-1-931968-43-0 (pbk. : alk. paper)
1. Akron (Ohio)—Tours. 2. Historic sites—Ohio—Akron—
Guidebooks. 3. Walking—Ohio—Akron—Guidebooks.
I. Ayers, Chuck (Charles W.) II. Title.
F499.A3M87 2007
977.1´36—dc22
2006039284

Book design and composition by Kachergis Book Design

Contents

List of Illustrations

Walks around Akron

The windmill-topped washhouse (center), the covered well, and porch column dominate this backyard view of the Summit County Historical Society's Perkins Stone Mansion.

List of Illustrations   ix

Preface

The idea that grew into this book was born on a long walk along East Exchange Street in Akron, Ohio, in 1987. I had dropped off my car for service at a garage near the eastern terminus of Exchange and was hiking back to work downtown at the *Akron Beacon Journal*. What I saw along the way surprised me, even though I had driven this stretch of road countless times before.

That's when it hit me: I was always so hurried in my travels that I tended to look at but seldom really see the world around me. I proposed this as the theme for a story in the *Beacon* magazine. Ann Sheldon Mezger, then editor of the magazine, had a better idea. She envisioned a monthly feature, rather than a single story. And instead of having a photographer illustrate each article, she elected to have artist Chuck Ayers walk with me, with his sketchpad in hand.

That was the beginning of our series about the simple pleasures of walking. Our premise was simple: Take a walk in the community, then share what we saw with our readers. We soon discovered that Chuck wasn't illustrating my stories, but rather presenting visual essays to go along with my words. The series never had a name, but if our editors had insisted on one, "discovery" would have been a part of it, because even the most familiar places we visited yielded information that was new to us.

Our walks were featured in the newspaper from March 1987 through December 2000. The series ended three months shy of its fourteenth anniversary. We had always tried to focus on the yesterday-today-and-tomorrow aspect of the places we visited. As the new century began, we planned to zero in on places where things happened one hundred years ago and show them as they were then and are today. We have been able to do some of that since the feature resumed in *Akron City*, the magazine published three times a year by the city of Akron.

Akron is a city in transition, and many of the places shown in Chuck's illustrations disappeared from the landscape or were forever altered, often in the name of redevelopment, soon after the articles were published. After decades of neglect, the downtown area has been the scene of major redevelopment efforts that have significantly changed the face of the city. At the same time, the zoo has seen an infusion of funding and the University of Akron campus has been significantly altered by new buildings, the closing of streets, and landscaping designed to give a street-corner university a more traditional feel.

Other striking examples include the former B.F. Goodrich complex at the south end of downtown, which has been transformed from an eyesore into a hub of activity, featuring corporate headquarters and a business incubator; the redevelopment of the Ohio & Erie Canal towpath trail; the ongoing improvements to the park system; and plans for the restoration and reuse of the Howe House, which has stood at East Exchange and South High streets since 1836.

Reflecting on our work as we pulled this book together, we realized we had inadvertently documented the community in transition and that transition is at the heart of this book. At the same time we recognize that our stories, like snapshots in a family album, depict places that have drastically changed and people who have moved on or died since the material was initially published. We've updated stories wherever possible and apologize for any we have missed.

Walks around Akron

CHAPTER ONE

Old Akron

One building cannot tell the whole story of a city, but the Howe House, standing at the southwest corner of East Exchange and South High streets, speaks volumes about Akron from its earliest days to the present. I expressed that sentiment in this article.

JULY 9, 2000

Howe House, Then and Now

A green space alien stared back at us from the back wall of the graffiti-scarred Akron landmark. Artist Chuck Ayers and I didn't realize how significant the building was until we visited the place armed with information provided by the city of Akron and ninety-one-year-old Nina Howe Stanford of Boston Township, a great-granddaughter of its builder, Captain Richard Howe, the engineer who laid out the Ohio & Erie Canal between Cleveland and Massillon.

We examined the house from every imaginable angle, beginning at the back, in the new parking lot that wraps around the south and west sides of the building. Graffiti spraypainted on the walls and rear doors informed us that "LA'ROX HAS MOVED" and—just above the green space alien—

I

"WE'RE OUT THERE." The irony of the vandalism that produced the graffiti is that the boarded-up building once was the home of two Akron law enforcement officials—Summit County Sheriff Jacob Chisnell, who rented it from Captain Howe's oldest daughter, Emily B. Ingersoll, in 1875, and Akron Police Chief John Durkin, who bought it in 1900 from Howe descendants. Chuck and I knew about Durkin's ownership, but neither of us had ever heard of Chisnell before Mrs. Stanford shared some family history and Akron officials let us read the Howe House Historic Structure Report prepared by the Cuyahoga Valley National Recreation Area's technical assistance and professional services division.

The Chisnells—the sheriff's wife wasn't identified by name—had nine children, and their home became the center of Akron's social life. Newt Chisnell, the oldest son, directed a drama group, the Emmet Club, from the home until he became a well-known touring actor. That's all according to the report, which was based on a study conducted when the National Park Service was considering a proposal to move Howe House a couple of blocks to the west, to Lock 1 of the canal. Such a move has been deemed infeasible, and now the city of Akron, which owns the building, is exploring options for its restoration or renovation.

Howe House is said to have been the first brick house built in Akron and was called the city's first mansion in a series published in the *Akron Times-Press* in 1936, the building's centennial year. It was built on Lot 154 of the original Connecticut Land Company survey of the Western Reserve. The Howe House report traces the lot's ownership from 1799, when John Kinsman bought a large tract of what would become Akron from the land company. Kinsman sold the property to Joseph Perkins, General Simon Perkins's cousin, in 1808, and four years later Perkins sold 109 acres—including Lot 154—to Paul Williams.

In his book, *Yesterday's Akron: The First 150 Years,* Kenneth Nichols described Williams as General Perkins's "necessary if over-shadowed partner" in the platting of Akron in December 1825 because he owned part of the land and was "the head of the only family living within the boundaries."

A contemporary view of Howe House contrasts with (inset) how it appeared in 1920 when seen from Main and Exchange Streets.

Captain Howe had been resident engineer for the canal's northern division five years when he bought Lot 154 from Williams on April 4, 1830. He and his wife, the former Roxana Jones, were living on a four-hundred acre farm on the Cuyahoga River in what was then Northampton Township. Their seven children included a son, Henry, Mrs. Stanford's grandfather, who would become a member of the Akron Board of Education. In 1835, Captain Howe hired James McMillen of Carroll County to build a sixteen-room brick house on Lot 154. By then he had also purchased Lot 155 next door and maintained a barn behind the house on Lot 156. Tax records for 1837 indicate the house was completed in 1836 and was valued at $1,400.

The Howes moved into the house in 1837. They boarded a schoolteacher and paid her salary so their children would get an education, Mrs. Stanford said. In 1840, Captain Howe donated use of a building to house a school in Akron's fledgling education system.

Captain Howe resigned his commission as resident engineer in 1850, and led a forty-wagon convoy of 350 Akron residents to California in search of gold. That quest proved fruitless, but Howe found work as an engineer for the U.S. government. One of his jobs was plotting the baseline from Mount Diablo in California to the Pacific Ocean, which provided a surveying guide for plotting property in the state in the twentieth century.

Howe returned to his Akron home two years later and lived there until his death on March 18, 1872. His obituary listed, among his contributions, helping to route the Pennsylvania & Ohio Canal through Akron, helping to start the Akron Rural Cemetery (now Glendale), raising money for the first Summit County Courthouse and Jail, and being a founding member of the First German Reformed Church.

Emily B. Ingersoll inherited Howe House after her mother, Roxana Jones Howe, died on February 14, 1875, and rented it to the Chisnells, who lived there until 1894. Hard times—a depression in 1890 and the Panic of 1893—forced one of Captain Howe's daughters, Mary Anna, and her husband, John Wolf, once a prosperous dry goods merchant, to move back to the homestead. Ownership was transferred to the Wolfs, who lived there with their two sons for six years, until the Michigan Mutual Life Insurance Company repossessed the house on February 14, 1900.

Police Chief Durkin, who bought the house from Michigan Mutual that year, lived there until 1926, when it became too large for his family. He rented it to Peter Culurianos, a Greek immigrant, who moved his family to the second floor and built a storefront at street level for his produce business. The neighborhood changed a lot during those twenty-six years. The German-American Music Hall, built in 1904 across the street at 44 East Exchange, was torn down in 1929 for construction of the *Akron Times-Press* building. A few doors to the west on Exchange, the Akron, Canton & Youngstown Railroad built an office tower in 1919.

Culurianos closed the business in the depression year of 1938, but Durkin kept the building. The Beacon Candy Shoppe opened there in 1939, named for the *Akron Beacon Journal,* which had moved into the building at 44 East Exchange after it bought the *Times-Press.*

Howe House remained in the Durkin family until 1947, when one of the police chief's descendants sold it to John Despotes, also a Greek immigrant, who lived upstairs and rented the commercial space below until his death on August 31, 1965. Ownership passed to his brother and sister-in-law, John and Marie Despotes, who rented the building to a variety of commercial ventures until the city of Akron bought it and the surrounding property in 1998.

Our on-site inspection tour proved less interesting than the historical one, until Chuck came up with the idea of showing Howe House before the storefront was added. We pored over old photos, marveling at some in which billboards on the roof of the storefront totally hid the residence from view. In the end, the artist chose the year 1920 for his illustration because the Howe House is shown flanked by the German-American Music Hall and the brand new AC&Y building.

6 ❧ Old Akron

AUGUST 1, 1993

The Length and Breadth of Old Akron

Old maps and imagination were our basic tools as we set out to explore old Akron. That's "old" as in original. Akron as platted by Joshua Henshaw in 1825 consisted of 302 numbered parcels bisected by the Ohio & Erie Canal. The original village boundaries were just north of what is now State Street on the north, just east of what is now Broadway on the east, and just west of what is now Locust Street on the west. The southern boundary is a bit tougher to describe because two canal basins occupied the southeast corner of Akron approximately from what is now Water Street and Wooster Avenue on the west to Selle Street and Broadway on the east.

The most remarkable thing we discovered during this exercise was not how much has changed in 168 years but how much remains the same. Akron's streets were unnamed in the original plat, but they were planned, nonetheless, as part of a community that founders General Simon Perkins and Paul Williams envisioned would serve the commercial trade developed by the canal. The thoroughfares that became State, Buchtel, Exchange, Cedar, Main, and Broadway were sketched in at one-hundred-and-fifty chain links. That's ninety-nine feet if the map was referring to surveyors' chain, or one-hundred-and-fifty feet if the reference was to engineers' chain. (The map-maker didn't specify which, but one-hundred surveyors' links equal sixty-six feet, and engineers' links each measure a foot.)

High and Broadway dead-ended at the canal basin, just south of Selle, and Main stopped a block north of that at Cedar, with the land between Cedar and the basin labeled "public ground." This is not to be confused with Public Square, an entity from Akron's inception that can still be seen today. In fact, its original boundary is newly marked in brick in front of Children's Hospital. The square was originally bounded by Buchtel, Bowery, Exchange, and Locust, and was for years called Perkins Square in honor of the founder.

The Buchtel section of the boundary is now part of the expanded hospi-

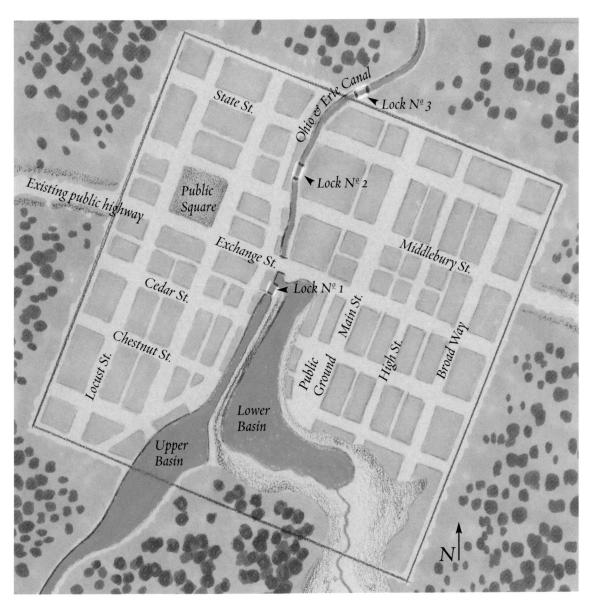

State St.

Ohio & Erie Canal

Lock Nº 3

Lock Nº 2

Existing public highway

Public Square

Exchange St.

Middlebury St.

Cedar St.

Lock Nº 1

Main St.

Chestnut St.

Public Ground

High St.

Broad Way

Locust St.

Lower Basin

Upper Basin

N

Map of the original plat for Akron shows the Ohio & Erie Canal, Locks 1 and 2, the two canal basins, and Public Square.

tal, but the brick border was added to permanently label the city landmark. Each corner of the boundary bears a brass seal that reads: "Public Square property corner. Platted December 6, 1825."

If the square was the most public of the sights we saw, the least was near the southeast corner of the original village of Akron. We started by getting an overview from the crest of the Exchange Street bridge that spans the railroad tracks just east of Broadway. Looking south at the embankment behind the old Erie depot, we could see old Akron's eastern border clearly defined. We took the sidewalk in front of the depot south along Broadway to Selle, then detoured along the old railroad tracks, past rusting old switches and decomposing railroad ties.

Through the scrub brush, we found a beehive of activity; cement trucks were being loaded just below and to the west of the bridge that carries Broadway over the lowland. As we watched, it occurred to us that the area we were looking at would have been part of the canal basin. From our vantage point, we could see the High Street bridge and what's beneath it. In the background, we also could see the Spaghetti Warehouse, the newest reuse project in the old B. F. Goodrich complex.

We crossed the former basin walking west along Selle, pausing briefly to listen to the pounding rhythm of machines at work inside the Akron Selle Company before moving on to Main Street. We cut across the weeds in a vacant lot at the north end of the B. F. Goodrich complex and slid down an embankment to get to the stub of Orleans Street beneath the Cedar Street bridge, which bore a spray-painted testimonial to Motley Crüe and condemnation of someone named Rochelle. Good taste prohibits direct quotation.

Through the trees, vines, and brush, we could see the canal, but just barely, and across to the west a cluster of buildings dominated by the back side of the Cotter warehouse. From our spot, the buildings seemed closer together than they actually are, as we discovered later when we reached the west end of the plat. We got there by walking north along Orleans to Exchange Street, chuckling at a sign at the M & M Electric Company. It read: "Let an electrician check your shorts." The buildings on the east side of Orleans all front on Main Street, but the rear view is equally impressive. Chuck recalled sketching the backs of the buildings from the bridge when he was a student.

Just around the corner from Orleans, we crossed over Lock 1 of the canal and the Ohio Department of Natural Resources hydraulic operations station. That's on the south side of Exchange. To the north, below the bridge, we found a shaded, placid sight, complete with a couple of swimming ducks.

From the west end of the plat, across the Public Square, on the site of Chuck's alma mater, Hower High School, we looked back from where we had come and marveled at the bowl shape of the original village of Akron. We were at Locust and Exchange on the lip of a bowl that dipped downhill to the canal, then up again to the high ground at Broadway.

Here is where imagination came in handy. Surrounded by pavement and buildings, we wondered what the land might have looked like as Henshaw began his plat. Then it occurred to us that we already knew what it looked like—or approximately so. All we had to do was look around us in any direction at the all-green skyline.

We concluded our look at old Akron from the roof of the *Beacon Journal* parking deck, from which we could see virtually the whole plat. It also was the perfect location from which to sketch one of Akron's oldest buildings, the Howe House.

JUNE 5, 1994

From the Summit to the Bluff

Virtually everything we looked at was a reminder of Akron as it used to be. The focus of our walk was College Street from Buchtel Common to the bluff of the Little Cuyahoga River Valley.

The traffic circle at the southern terminus of College is the staging area for the annual motorcade to the West Akron grave of Dr. Bob Smith, who, with New York businessman Bill Wilson, founded Alcoholics Anonymous in 1935. AA members from all over the world gather on the University of Akron campus each June to celebrate the organization's founding and their ongoing struggles for sobriety. The motorcade, an impressive mixture of motorcycles, cars, and buses, for all intents and purposes closes the weekend gathering.

An ornate iron fence along the College and Mill Street sides of Central-Hower High School obviously predates the school's 1970s construction. A search through old *Beacon Journal* photos revealed that the fence originally surrounded a triangular-shaped park bordered by College, Mill, and Forge streets in front of the original Central High School. Today the park is the school's front lawn.

Looking west along Forge toward downtown Akron, the Summit County Courthouse could be seen in the background and Wonder Bread silos rose over the roof of Michael Trecaso's restaurant. We paused to admire the First Methodist Church, which Chuck's family began attending when his father, Charles W. Ayers Sr., was a child and lived on College Street. A few days after our walk, fire destroyed the church.

College Street takes a forty-five-degree turn at Mill, and it appeared that we left the university behind as we approached the Goodwill Industries headquarters (now the University of Akron's Student Services Building), which has the legend "THE SUMMIT WHOLESALE GROCERY COMPANY" etched into its white stone finish. The Akron Community Service and Urban League headquarters across the street is another example of adaptive reuse of an older building.

Until 1950, College Street led to Akron's Union Station, which stood for fifty-nine years in the railroad valley just north of East Market Street. Before crossing Market, we stopped to inspect the old railroad signal house that Chuck recalled from his youth. It stands at the southwest corner of College and Market and looks rather unremarkable from the street. From the Market Street bridge, we could see that the building and its neighbors stand on sandstone foundations that extend two and three stories below street level. The area below and south of the bridge is a cemetery for old tires. A plaque on the bridge dates it as a 1939 project of the Federal Works Agency of the Public Works Administration.

This gatepost is all that remained of the old Union Station.

We crossed Market to study the Union Station site, which was littered with two-liter beer and wine bottles, many still wrapped in their brown bags. The site looked nothing like old photos in the *Beacon Journal* reference library. The only remnant of the station was an ornate iron post at the bottom of a ramp and stairs to Market Street. The post was painted a garish yellow and green. A 1905 photo showed that an iron banister ran the length of the ramp and stairs to the post. The photo caption indicated that the station was built in 1891 on what had been the George D. Bates homestead.

The area behind the station was known as Amelia Flats and was the site of the Grace Park Apartments. The word AKRON was spelled out in flowers or shrubs on the grassy slope leading up to the apartments. An unmarked cobblestone street runs alongside the sandstone ramp for part of the way down to the tracks. Then it just ends, the result of a rather informal landfill operation that has taken place in the forty-three years since the depot was demolished.

The clock tower of the First Congregational Church, visible through the trees, and the twin spires of St. Bernard's Catholic Church reminded us we weren't far from home base. We walked up a service road to Grace Park, where a woman and six small children were having a picnic lunch. The park, we discovered, is fenced by the same ornate iron we saw at Central-Hower.

The service road ends at a permanent barricade at Perkins Street, and College Street resumes for one more block. Modern apartments and older homes line the short street, as they do Bluff Street, named for obvious reasons. At 277 Bluff, we made the discovery that makes these walks so much fun. Some would call it an old brick building. A child might prefer to think of it as an old castle. Owner John Kropac calls it the Dolly Madison Mattress and Box Spring Company, a family business operated by his father, Rudolph, eighty-five, until he retired ten years ago. The four-story tower, which gives the building its distinctive look, has no practical value, Kropac said. The previous owner put lavatories in the lower levels, but there isn't any way to get to the top floor, he said. Kropac invited us inside to see the original blueprints, which date to 1870. The building was built as part of the Pflueger manufacturing complex, which dominated that section of Akron in the last century.

At the Curve on Main

Time doesn't exactly stand still on Old Main Street in Akron. But it does seem to have slowed down a bit. If you've never heard of Old Main Street, don't apologize. Neither had we before a friend took a wrong turn and found herself staring at the faded printing on the front of a building at Ira Avenue and Old Main. A Parasson's restaurant, perhaps the first, featured steaks and chops, according to the faded legend. Our friend encouraged us to take a hike to see the place for ourselves. We did and discovered—again—that things are seldom what they appear to be.

Old Main begins at Miller Avenue, where South Main Street takes a southeasterly turn to meet the southerly terminus of Broadway. It ends a block to the south, where it meets Ira Avenue at another curve in the road. Old Main is clearly marked as such, but I had never noticed it on those occasions when I drove along its course to get to the east end of Kenmore Boulevard. In fact, I had never noticed the Ira Avenue signs until our recent visit. I guess I thought Kenmore began at the Main Street curve.

The buildings along Old Main Street are mostly two- and three-story, with stores on the first floors and apartments above. The upper stories looked mostly vacant, although brothers Dwight and John Frame said many of the apartments have tenants. The Frames were doing some repair work to the front of their business, D & J Used Furniture and Appliance at 1151 Old Main. It is one of the three used-furniture businesses on the block. Dwight Frame said he has seven residential tenants, as well as people who rent storage space in his buildings.

Other businesses on the block include Ton Yee Laundry and the Fil-Mar Products Company, both of which have signs, and a grocery store that has no sign and doesn't need one, according to owners Cato and Nola Smith. The Smiths specialize in Southern specialties such as collard, turnip and mustard greens, black-eyed peas, and other produce grown on their seventy-acre farm in Rootstown, plus brands of canned and packaged groceries not carried by the larger stores. Customers drive in from Pittsburgh and Chicago just for the salt pork, Cato Smith said.

The store is at 5 Ira Avenue in the building that was once occupied by Parasson's. The Smiths opened for business there in May after operating the Bellows Cash Market at Miller and Bellows Avenues for forty-seven years. The tiny store looks as if it could have been transplanted from a rural cross-roads. Shelves line the side walls and produce is displayed in baskets in front of the meat case. Customer Thomas Flippen said he followed the Smiths to their new location.

Their landlord is ninety-two-year-old Jacob Mallo, whose wife, Grace, is Cato Smith's sister. The Mallos happened to be visiting the morning we were there. Jacob Mallo recalled with pride that he sold the *Beacon Journal* as a teenager. With equal pride, he pointed out that his son, Ted, is counsel for the University of Akron. Mallo has owned the building since 1947. He said it previously housed two hotels, the Earl and the Firestone, as well as a jewelry store and barbershop. His wife also operated an antique shop there for ten years. A bridge used to carry Main Street across the railroad tracks to the front of the Firestone complex, Grace Mallo said.

Chuck found his vantage point across the street from the grocery store. From there, he had a good view of Jacob Mallo's trapezoid-shaped building (it has no right angles) and a picturesque lot that separates it from the first building on Old Main. At the rear of the lot is a flight of stairs leading to the next street. The artist also was taken by the row of buildings on the east side of Old Main, especially the one at 1157. It stands next to another vacant lot and is partially covered by shingles along its south side. The rest of that side was previously covered by another building, which, when razed, left a telltale section of unpainted wooden siding.

The buildings at the south end of Old Main are warehouses for used home appliances. A sign on the wall of one of them marks the parking space for the pastor of the Saints Temple First Born Church of the Living God at 1162 Old Main. The parking space was empty when we arrived, but it was occupied when I left the grocery store, so I decided to visit the sanctuary. The Reverend Ellis McKenzie seemed surprised to have a weekday visitor, although he said people from the neighborhood occasionally drop in for counseling. He said his 125-member congregation moved to the tiny building at Lake and Old Main eight years ago, after the city bought the church's former location at 189 Abel Street. A restaurant previously occupied the portion of the building that fronts on Lake, and a furniture store was in the Old Main section, McKenzie said.

JUNE 1, 1997

Hidden in Plain Sight

Graffiti and litter competed for attention with fragrant lilacs and sweet-sounding birds on our successful search for the John Brown monument in Akron's Perkins Park. The memorial to the abolitionist, who spent his early years in Hudson and herded sheep in Akron before his day of destiny at the Harpers Ferry government arsenal, stands in a clearing bordered by the high trees above the park's tennis courts and the fence that confines the Akron Zoological Park.

That much we knew from conversations with retired Ohio Edison attorney Frances McGovern (now deceased) and naturalist Joe Jesensky, and from reading local history perspectives by the late Margot Jackson who, in 1991, described the monument as "probably the least visited structure in the city." And no wonder. If you know it's there, it's visible, but just barely from the street on the west side of the park on Perkins Park Drive. It can't be seen at all from the east side on Edgewood Avenue, at least not when the trees are in bloom.

Following directions from McGovern and Jesensky, Chuck and I parked at the Ed Davis Community Center on Perkins Park Drive and went looking for the driveway that cuts through Edgewood. Our search took us along a stretch of sidewalk so new we were tempted to touch it for hardness. The sidewalk bore the imprint "Vito Gironda Brothers," as well as the date, 1996, and the company telephone number. New grass grew thickly though layers of straw on either side for as far as we could see.

We passed a hill where, Chuck recalled, he had gone sledding with his brother during the winter when he was five and Mike was two-and-a-half. The John Brown monument was just yards away through the trees, but we had to take that on faith. We still couldn't see it. And if anyone had told Chuck about it when he was a child, he couldn't remember.

Concrete barricades block the driveway to motor vehicles but not pedestrians or bicyclists, so we headed into the park, still not sure exactly where to look for the monument. No park signs marked the way, just empty wine and beer bottles and a few fast-food containers. The litter reminded me of the universality of the cleanup problem faced by city dwellers and suburbanites alike, especially in neighborhoods bordering parks and other gathering spots.

As we approached a magnificent oak, standing at least sixty feet tall at the drive's north edge, we spotted the monument off to our left. Gnarled bumps called burls decorated the tree trunk, and a nuthatch scampered along a branch forty feet above us. An empty Wild Irish Rose bottle at the bottom of the tree completed the still life and told us someone else had passed this way before.

We followed a footpath worn into the grass between the drive and the monument, pausing along the way to inspect eleven small markers that dotted the landscape. They were metal plaques dating from 1913 through the 1930s and affixed to large rocks and concrete bases, all in memory of founders and other members of the Akron and Summit County Home and School League, which, we later learned, evolved into the Parent-Teacher Association.

One of the plaques, which described the league as a "builder of high ideals through love, harmony, and education," bore pry marks from a failed attempt to remove it from its base, and another base rested on its back with only four metal anchors in the stone to indicate a plaque had ever been there.

The signs of vandalism were like a warm-up to the monument and its mixed messages of honor and dishonor. I won't dignify the specifics of the

The graffiti-covered monument to abolitionist John Brown stands in Perkins Park.

words and symbols we found sprayed in black paint on the monument and the sandstone octagon in which it stands—except for one. The word "THUG" seems an appropriate description of the person who sprayed it.

A stone wall at the back of the octagon bears a circular relief of John Brown's head and shoulders that someone has painted—not inartistically—in shades of red, orange, white and blue. Below it, etched in the sandstone, are "He Died to Set His Brothers Free" and "His Soul Goes Marching On" and "Dedicated Sept. 25, 1938 by the Negro 25-year-club of Akron, Ohio." It was the monument's second dedication. The first, according to a plaque on the monument, was August 21, 1910, when the German-American Alliance erected it, using a stone column from Summit County's original courthouse.

An eagle with outstretched wings topped the monument until a tornado blew it away on its destructive path through Akron in 1943, we later read in *At Home on the Hill: The Perkins Family In Akron,* the book Margot Jackson and her late husband, James Jackson, wrote for the Summit County Historical Society in 1983.

A .32-caliber shell casing Chuck found on the stone floor of the octagon was our signal to leave the carpet of leaves, litter, and broken glass.

Back on Perkins Park Drive, we stopped to admire another still life—some wildflowers decorated with another wine bottle, right behind a spray-painted Keep Akron Beautiful sign:

> You litter
> We fine
> $500

We walked to the end of the new sidewalk, specifically to see if the monument was visible from the road. It was, but not easily.

It was field-trip day at the zoo, and the parking lot below our vantage point was alive with children walking away from or toward their yellow school buses. Except for a lone stroller on the driveway near the monument, these were the first signs of life we saw, human or animal. And we were just outside the zoo.

Then three deer appeared out of nowhere, cautiously walking at a right angle from us within the safety of the fence and at least fifty feet away. One seemed to be the leader. It never took its eyes off us. When it moved, the others moved a few paces. When it stopped, the others did, too, waiting for the signal to continue.

We were diverted from this graceful procession by a tom turkey that fretted and paced along the fence line, puffing its feathers. We thought it was all for our benefit until Chuck followed its line of sight across Perkins Park Drive and spotted the head of another turkey—a female that flew the coop, we guessed—popping up and down in the foot-tall grass. When the escaped turkey's head came up, the incarcerated tom would puff and stretch; when it disappeared into the grass, the tom fretted and paced some more. We reported our turkey sighting to a zoo attendant, whose reaction suggested that runaways are not all that unusual.

Then we headed for the Perkins Stone Mansion at South Portage Path and Copley, where Paula Moran (then interim head, now executive director of the historical society) gave us permission to look inside the John Brown home across the street, which the abolitionist occupied from 1844 to 1846, when he worked for Simon Perkins Jr. I was surprised to learn that the house's many uses since then included being the clubhouse for Akron's first golf course, started in 1895 and incorporated as the Portage Country Club in 1904, when it moved to North Portage Path and Twin Oaks Road. The move was precipitated in part because Perkins's sons, George, who owned the land, and Charles, who owned the clubhouse, frowned upon playing golf on Sunday and the consumption of liquor, according to the Jacksons' book.

Lilacs blooming along the path across the Perkins Mansion lawn provided the perfect ending for our walk. We smelled them before we saw them.

Islands of the Past

It really feels weird to discover you're seeing the world from a new perspective. Literally. You're in familiar surroundings when, all of a sudden, you realize that the piece of real estate you're standing on was, until relatively recently, occupied by a building. The real estate in question was the parking lot at the northwest corner of Market and Main streets in downtown Akron. The building it replaced was the Portage Hotel, which stood there from 1912 to 1992. We parked in the lot so we could take a closer look at a sign that spelled out "CANAL ST" in white letters on a green background.

The street sign hangs from a utility pole at what had been the intersection of Canal and Market. All other traces of Canal Street are gone, replaced by a field in which weeds are winning a turf war with the grass. Gone, too, is any indication that Howard Street ever intersected Market. Our copy of an 1870 Akron map showed Canal Street running parallel with Howard from one block north of Furnace Street, near the Ohio & Erie Canal's Lock 13, south to Mill Street, near Locks 6 and 5. Canal ended at Mill in 1870, while Howard continued at a southeasterly angle, joining Main Street to form what was known as the Flatiron block. The section of Howard and Canal south of Market disappeared during the downtown redevelopment of the 1960s and 1970s.

Using the old map, we calculated that my car was parked where Howard once ran along the back side of the Portage Hotel, which stood on the site of an earlier hotel, the Empire House. Karl H. Grismer's *Akron and Summit County* and other references had told us that the Empire, built in 1847, was considered premier among several hotels that went up along the canal.

We started north across the weeds toward Martin Luther King Jr. Boulevard, that short, curved roadway linking Perkins Street with the Martin Luther King Jr. Expressway (a.k.a. the Innerbelt). Looking back toward Market, Chuck found the perspective for his first illustration, which shows blue-

The sign was all that remained of Canal Street when we looked south along West Market Street at what had been the heart of the original Akron.

painted utility stacks rising through weeds, juxtaposed against the Federal, Bank One, First Energy, 1 Cascade Plaza, and Radisson Hotel Akron buildings to the south. He pointed out that we were standing on what had been the path of a rail line that ran between the canal and Canal Street.

The weed field was strewn with broken pieces of red brick, which we guessed came either from the old pavement or long-gone buildings, or possibly both. As we approached the north end of the field, we noticed that utility poles and the lines they carry over Martin Luther King Boulevard and through the trees to the north marked the path Canal Street had once followed. To get to the other side of those trees, we climbed a grassy hill to the sidewalk at the Martin Luther King Boulevard-Main-Howard convergence, pausing while we waited for the traffic light to change to admire the small stand of pine trees and bed of flowers planted by members of Keep Akron Beautiful.

The short block between the boulevard and Beech Street is occupied by a building at 10 North Howard that bears a sign identifying it as the Interbelt Nite Club. We walked west on Beech and soon came to another white-on-green Canal Street sign. This time there was a street to go with it—a stub, really, paved with gravel and/or cinders and running beneath an old trestle that carries the Cuyahoga Valley Scenic Railroad into downtown Akron.

At the end of the street stood an old house, painted emerald green and trimmed in purple and reddish brown. That became the focus of Chuck's second illustration. It's the same house that looks down on the intersection of Howard and Furnace, at the north end of what I call the "Main Street Island," that section of Main between Furnace and Perkins that was isolated when the Y-shaped All-America Bridge was built. I spoke to owner Aggie Russell (now deceased) after our walk. Russell, reached by phone, said her plans for the one-hundred-year-old house, which she called "The Painted Lady," will depend on what happens to property on the Main Street Island. "I'll have to go with the flow," Russell said. "We'll be part of what's happening on the Main Street. I'm happy to be a part of it. If you ever go by and see a little old lady pushing a lawn mower, that'll be me." ("The Painted Lady" was demolished in 2004 after arsonists damaged it beyond repair.)

We decided to climb the hill to the trestle to see if it afforded a better perspective. It didn't because the walls are too high. But our detour east along the tracks led us to another grassy field, where we stumbled on another piece of Akron history. The field is at the south end of the Main Street Island. We were attracted to it by the red and black metal sculptures on display with no signage to indicate their source. Nearby, black-eyed Susans and blue cornflowers grew in a small plot ringed by small rocks and marked with a hand-lettered quotation attributed to the book of Proverbs in the Bible: "The gift is a stone winning favor in the eyes of its grand owner. Everywhere he turns he has success."

As we pondered the story behind the sculptures and the flowers, two men showed up to discuss, we soon learned, plans for a public art project to celebrate the history of the Mathew Hotel, which once stood on Howard adjacent to the trestle and where Louis Armstrong, Cab Calloway, and Ella Fitzgerald, among other African American entertainers, once stayed and performed. The men were Akron artist Miller Horns, who is spearheading the project, and Joe Scaccio, president of the Carmen Construction Company, the general contractor. They said they were laying out preliminary plans for a sidewalk and ramp for the disabled that will lead to the memorial, which will occupy the hotel site.

JANUARY 1, 1999

Walk in Old Middlebury Is a Fountain of History

From a distance, the old carriage house at Crouse and Forrest Streets in East Akron looks pretty good. The weathervane still turns when the wind blows, and you don't notice the holes in the roof and some of its windows. But up close, the red brick remnant of another era looks as if it could use a new lease on life. Whether it gets one depends on the findings of a study being conducted by its new owner, Oriana House, a private, nonprofit community corrections agency.

We didn't know who owned the carriage house when we visited the neighborhood landmark. All we knew was that it had been part of industrial pioneer David E. Hill's property at Arlington and Crouse Streets. A sign on the lawn near the sidewalk along Arlington suggested the owner was American Legion Post 209. We parked in the brick alley next to the carriage house, which stands at the northeast corner of the former Hill estate. The alley ended at a circle that was a traffic turnaround by design or simply usage. The Legion headquarters, a second, newer building at the southeast corner, was boarded up.

The four-story Hill mansion, so described in local histories, had stood in the expanse between the alley and Arlington, although no signs of the building remain today. Hill lived there when he operated a sewer pipe company that bore his name. And he lived there when F. A. Seiberling was seeking investors for his new company, Goodyear. Hill's purchase of $30,000 in Goodyear stock—$20,000 for himself and $10,000 for a son—earned him the first company presidency in 1898. He resigned a year later and was succeeded by another investor, R. C. Penfield of Willoughby, who was Seiberling's brother-in-law. Seiberling, who was Goodyear's general manager at the start, went on to become its fourth president in 1906.

A low sandstone wall along the Arlington side of the property and pink and gray sandstone pillars mark the entrances to two curved sandstone walkways that lead from the sidewalk to what had been the front of the mansion. In a neighboring building south of the Legion post, we discovered the new home of a tattoo and piercing parlor that had been the *Akron Beacon Journal's* neighbor at High and Exchange Streets until last year.

A steeple atop the carriage house gives that building a churchlike appearance, although the large horseshoe-shaped front window more accurately hinted at its actual use. Still, it looks right at home with its neighbors at Arlington and Crouse—the Middlebury Chapel and St. Mary Orthodox Church. The weathervane was turning in the wind atop the steeple, which had lost more than a few of its roofing shingles and, if there had ever been one, its bell.

We learned from a local history that Hill's first job after he came to Mid-

The carriage house of the former David Hill mansion was razed in 1999.

dlebury from Gowanda, New York, in 1843 was in a machine shop that made fire engines. We wondered whether his carriage house was a reflection of the fire stations of that era. After all, it was Hill who provided the cast-iron fountain—a statue of two small children under an umbrella—that graces the center of the tiny wading pool in Middlebury Square Park nearby at East Market and East Exchange Streets. We learned about that fountain on our first walk around the neighborhood in May 1988. The fountain was missing; Akron firefighters from Station No. 2 adjacent to the park, who have cared for it for years, told us it was away for repairs. It was back a year later when the late Margot Jackson, in a *Beacon Journal* article, called it the oldest fountain in Akron, about one hundred years old.

At age twenty-four, Hill tapped into the burgeoning clay products industry, organizing the Akron Sewer Pipe Company in 1849 and the Hill Sewer Pipe Company in 1873. He was a Republican Party member from its earliest days, and an officerholder—Summit County commissioner from 1862 to 1868, Middlebury school board member until the village was annexed to Akron in 1872, and Akron Sixth Ward council member from 1875 to 1878. The Akron public schools named an elementary school after David Hill, so the name remains familiar even if details of the man's contributions blur with time.

American Legion Post 209 commander Jacob Yates, financial officer Wayne Wright, and Oriana House executive vice president Bernie Rochford filled in a few blanks in our story, but they, too, wished they knew more. The Legion post started elsewhere in 1919 and then met in the old four-story mansion from 1926, when it bought the Hill property for $6,000, until its new building opened in 1954, Wright said. The carriage house was used as a rifle range for many years and then was leased to a dog trainer until he died in the 1980s. The property was sold to Oriana House last spring because post membership had been dwindling and a smaller building was found on Brown Street, Yates said.

Rochford said Oriana House will use the former Legion post building for storage for the immediate future and eventually will renovate it, adding a kitchen, and use it for staff development and training. "We're in the midst of evaluating the property," Rochford said. "There's plenty of parking and good expansion space." The evaluation will include the carriage house, but he said he fears it may not be feasible to save. (He was right; it was razed.)

AUGUST 13, 2000

Behind the Eight Ball

Weeds and wildflowers—Queen Anne's lace, black-eyed Susans, and cornflowers—grew tall down the middle of the unused railroad siding just outside the southwestern gate of the sprawling acreage that is home to the Akron Fulton International Airport, the University of Akron's Rubber Bowl, Derby Downs, and Lockheed Martin's Akron Tactical Defense Systems operations. Before us, on the opposite side of a tall chain-link fence, loomed the Airdock, Lockheed Martin's since 1996 and Loral's for nine years before that, but still associated in the minds of many with Goodyear, which built it in 1929.

It was memories of Goodyear and its round-the-clock World War II production efforts that brought us to the south end of the property on a hot summer morning. The memories belong to our parents' generation. I was seven when the war ended—fifty-five years ago tomorrow on August 14, 1945—and Chuck hadn't been born. But we both grew up hearing stories—snippets, really—about our parents' wartime experiences.

Chuck's mother, the former Gertrude McPeek, was among the thousands of women who donned work clothes and took over the production-line spots of the American men who went off to war. Immortalized in the Rosie-the-Riveter cartoons of the era, these women built parts for the tanks, planes, and other weaponry that defeated the enemy. At the Goodyear Aircraft Corporation, Mrs. Ayers was part of the team that riveted tail assemblies for B-29 Super Fortress bombers in one of the sprawling factories that surround the Airdock. Another of her jobs, while her husband, Charles W. Ayers, served in the Army Air Force, was sealing the seams of barrage balloons.

In his history *Yesterday's Akron: The First 150 Years,* Kenneth Nichols said of

The Airdock looms in the background.

the war years: "'Tire Town' belied its name by becoming a major producer of airships, aircraft parts, complete fighter planes, and anti-aircraft guns—while turning out record numbers of military tires, tank tracks, bullet-sealing fuel tanks, and scores of other articles fashioned from 'man-made' rubber.... Akron became a twenty-four-hour town turned upside down. Women 'manned' factory machines; night clubs were open in daylight hours; and restaurants served dinner at six in the morning to swing shifters."

Nichols was writing about the efforts of all Akron-based rubber companies, but it was the women of Goodyear Aircraft who were pictured in his book, joyfully showering the factory with confetti made from waste papers in celebration of V-E Day, May 7, 1945, when the hostilities ended in Europe. The celebration was even bigger on V-J Day, August 14, when Japan surrendered, ending the fighting in Asia.

Goodyear Aircraft, which began as Goodyear Zeppelin Corporation and evolved into Goodyear Aerospace, had two thousand workers building military plane tail assemblies more than a year before the United States entered the war. By April 1941, three plants were turning out parts for four planes, the Martin B-26 medium bomber, the Consolidated four-motored heavy bomber, the Grumman Navy fighter, and the Curtiss P-40 Army Pursuit ship.

A news story dated August 12, 1942 said when the B-26C "roared into the air . . . on its first test flight, its wings, ailerons and tail surfaces represented the work of men and women on Goodyear Aircraft production lines...." Also in August 1942, the workers won a commendation from the War Production Board for the company's Eight Ball campaign to help produce one plane every eight minutes. The workers received Eight Ball pins and copies of a letter in which board chairman Donald M. Nelson praised them for increasing production by more than 10 percent: "Only by such an effort will the United States be able to take the offensive which is certain to put Hitler, Hirohito and Mussolini behind the eight ball. The worker on the production line has as important a place in this total war as the men in the services."

Other Goodyear Aircraft output during the war included a variety of parts for the Northrop P-61 Black Widow, three Grumman planes (the F6F Hellcat, F7F, and TBF Avenger), two Lockheed planes (the P-38 Lightning and PV2 Ventura), and the Martin PBM Mariner. In addition, the firm produced 3,700 Corsair fighters and more than 150 lighter-than-air craft for the U.S. Navy.

On July 28, 1945, two and a half weeks before the war ended, Goodyear Aircraft achieved a production milestone, the manufacture and shipment of its one hundred thousandth airplane part, a bomb bay section for the fuselage of a B-29. Russell De Young, then vice president in charge of production, was waiting at the end of the production line to congratulate his workers.

"No one realized when we started our first contract, how many more would be given us to do," De Young told the workers. "It looked like an impossible job, but you did it."

Chuck and I had just a vague idea of the Akron war effort when we walked along the fence looking at the Airdock. It took research afterward to help quantify it. But looking at a long row of semitrailers dwarfed by the seventy-one-year-old landmark, we knew it was the perfect symbol of the enormity of the workers' achievements.

CHAPTER TWO

The Changing Face
of Akron

*New buildings and old competed for our attention in eight forays around downtown
Akron during the late 1980s and through the 1990s. The common thread in each story
and illustration that resulted was change—a new building where none had been before,
a new use for a familiar landmark, or even a last look at a feature of the landscape that
was about to disappear.*

FEBRUARY 2, 1992

Walking Broadway

During my years in Akron, I have driven past the Old Stone School at
Broadway and East Buchtel Avenue almost daily. I often wondered about it,
but sitting behind the wheel I was never curious enough to stop and take the
time to learn. It took an approaching magazine deadline to stop the wheels
from turning and get the feet moving. The day was cold, with a wind-chill
factor of twelve degrees below zero, as Chuck and I headed north on Broadway from East Exchange Street. This, we decided, would be a short walk, a

31

few blocks to Quaker Square and back. If need be, we would scout the territory and return later to do our work. It didn't turn out that way. We found more to see and comment on than can be contained in one story. We've used the word "discovery" a lot during nearly five years of walking around Greater Akron. We'll use it again today, as we encourage you to park your car, take a walk, and discover your city. Take a camera along, unless you happen to know a good artist.

We hadn't thought about the old one-room schoolhouse when we set out, but Chuck knew it had to be part of his illustration as soon as he saw a group of children filing out of the building and onto their Akron school bus. With the University of Akron's polymer center looming in the background, the scene was a perfect symbol of the past, present, and future in Akron education. The school was built around 1840 and restored in 1967. It is owned by the Summit County Historical Society, which leases it to the Akron Board of Education. It stands on the site of Akron's first school building, which was destroyed by fire, and was the birthplace of the graded school system, according to old newspaper clippings and photos. In 1939 and 1942, the schoolhouse was the scene of reunions of former pupils who, in their twilight years, returned to reminisce about growing up in nineteenth-century Akron.

We didn't get to go inside, but a peek through the windows was enough to take us on a flight of fancy to an earlier time—until we got to the small addition at the rear of the building, where the view of a modern kitchen brought us back to the 1990s. The schoolhouse sits on the high ground on the west side of the railroad tracks that until recently separated the university from downtown Akron. Standing at the rear of the school site, we noticed for the first time that the land was terraced and had a driveway running behind it, below the Broadway street level and above the embankment leading to the tracks. Two dozen paces and one gentle curve later and we weren't downtown anymore. We might have been on an unpaved country lane, except for the incongruous sight of the *Beacon Journal* clock tower peeking at us from behind the roof line of the old schoolhouse. Peering over steel fencing intertwined with the roots of trees and shrubs, we looked north beyond the skywalk link-

Schoolchildren file out of the Old Stone School.

ing UA's main campus with the new business administration building on Broadway and decided to make the Amtrak station we spotted our final destination. We followed the driveway to the rear of a parking lot and found our way back to the sidewalk on Broadway.

At the business administration building, workmen on a scaffold were installing the exterior skin on the pedestrian skywalk that will link the new building with the former Polsky's parking deck on the other side of Broadway. They warmed to the fact that the wind-chill factor was low enough for them to quit for the day.

"These gals make me cold just looking at them," said one worker as some fashionably short-skirted students hurried into the building.

Chuck had never been inside the business administration building, so we took a tour, riding the glass-walled elevator to the top of the atrium and peering into some empty classrooms. The new skywalk was still off-limits, so we had to settle for the old one, which spans the tracks. From there we could pick out—but just barely—the rustic spot behind the old schoolhouse. We couldn't see the entrance to the Amtrak station, but we remembered seeing signs for it near the entrance to the Morley Health Center parking garage. So that's where we headed next.

The station entrance is just a few steps south of the Akron Hilton Inn (now the Crowne Plaza Akron) at Quaker Square. At an earlier time, before planes and interstate highways made rail travel all but obsolete, the train station would have been a jewel on the avenue. Today, it's a lonely platform between two sets of tracks, reached through a gate in a chain-link fence behind the health center. But from this cold and lonely platform one can see a city alive with activity. Looking south, we saw buses and trucks carrying traffic over University Boulevard (formerly Center Street) and Exchange Street. In between these two bridges was the skywalk we had just left. While we were there, two trains, long and heavy with freight, ground their way along the tracks.

Before the Scene Changes

The chilly day felt more like autumn than summer and the clouds threat-ened to douse us with rain, but we decided to hoof it anyway. It had been a year since we last walked in the rain. We were prompted by news on page one of the *Beacon Journal* that doomed our project—better make that "pipe dream." First, some background. We concluded our last adventure at South Broadway and East Exchange Street. If you were with us, you'll remember we were ogling the Goodyear blimp and gushing about planes and trains.

What we didn't share with readers was our fascination with the vacant Conrail station on the three-acre parcel owned by Akron lawyer Bob Meeker and being eyed by Flagship Properties of Cleveland, which wants to build $11.4 million worth of student housing there. We didn't know that at the time. We just saw a rather ordinary old train station that seemed, because of its proximity to the tracks and the Ohio & Erie Canal, to be the perfect loca-tion for a transportation museum. Most people, if they see the building at all, probably dismiss it as just another vacant structure. I had the advantage of studying it from behind, standing on what used to be a loading platform a level below Broadway. Part of the advantage was Chuck's memories of the station. Old photos show a skywalk that carried pedestrians from the station over the tracks to two stairways down to the boarding area.

We decided to give the readers one more look at the station before it is torn down. Chuck picked a spot on the Exchange Street bridge to offer two views of the Akron skyline as it is today, and at a time when rail transportation was still thriving. We then decided to check out another project that is chang-ing the city skyline, so we walked north on Broadway, then west on State Street toward Children's Hospital. Along the way, we noticed that the former Polsky's department store was a beehive of activity as workers made it ready to be the University of Akron's Main Street address. But we also stopped to smell the roses growing in the side and front yards of the incongruously resi-

Helicopter pad is seen from the top level of Children's Hospital parking deck.

dential setting of the ACCESS shelter house for homeless women and children. We paused on the State Street bridge over the canal to admire the red, orange, yellow, and lime-green wildflowers growing on the west bank.

People—almost as many as there were ducks in the water—were gathered at Lock 2 Park within the steel pipe construction shaped like an old canal boat. Several were reading from books or pamphlets, and one stood apart from the others and appeared to be reading to them as a teacher or preacher might. Just west of the park, we came to a place where a few years ago downtown condominiums were built and then razed to make room for the Children's Hospital expansion. The site had been vacant on our last visit. On this day, the foundation had been essentially completed and workmen were grading ramps for what appeared to be an underground parking garage.

Pausing at Bowery and State Streets, we enjoyed the vista looking east toward the UA Business Administration building, which was the vantage point for Chuck's *Angles and Arches* illustration. From there, Chuck noticed a charming deck with umbrella tables overlooking the canal from the rear of the Canal Park Tower, formerly the Akron Tower Motor Inn, at 50 West State.

We also witnessed a parade. At 3:45 P.M., the shift ended at the hospital construction site, and workers began to file out of the new wing, across Bowery, and through the park to their cars on the east side of the canal.

Grace United Church of Christ stands at the southwest corner of Bowery and State. It was on the horizon of Chuck's July illustration. Up close, it reprised the angles and arches theme even better. Four dates tell the church's construction story. It was built as Grace Reformed Church in 1853. Other buildings replaced the first in 1862 and 1881. The present building was erected in 1926. A sign informed us that the Reverend Stephanie Haines is pastor and that free lunches are served on Saturdays. The site, bordered by a lawn and hedges, is a peaceful oasis in the heart of bustle—a fact that didn't become apparent until we stepped beyond its boundaries. The back of the church abuts the parking lot atop the hospital emergency room. The sound level really increased as we moved away from the church. (The church has since been razed for more hospital expansion.)

We detoured into the hospital parking garage on Locust Street and took the elevator up to the roof to take in a sight I stumbled on while visiting a patient. An ivy-covered home stands in the shadow of the deck at West Buchtel Avenue and Pine Street, a dead-end brick-paved alley. We were looking down on the worn shingles of its roof, which was patched with long strips of equally worn tar paper. A flowery bush and two cars in the yard suggested this is home to at least a couple of people. We wondered if helicopters landing on the hospital pad just beyond the home ever disturb the occupants' sleep. (That home also was razed after this story was published.)

Then the clouds made good their threats and drenched us before we made it to shelter. But you already knew we were all wet.

FEBRUARY 7, 1993

Magical Mystery Tour

A hundred years from now someone will unearth a time capsule at 1 Perkins Square in Akron. That's a new address in 1993, as is the building it identifies, Children's Hospital Medical Center of Akron. Contents of the time capsule are known only to the committee that selected them. But that's okay. The secret only added to the allure of the eight-story building. It is the newest section of a hospital that has grown in size and scope for one hundred years.

The $75 million wing won't be completed until next month, and the first tours won't be scheduled for a couple of months, but Chuck and I found Bill Considine, hospital president, and Terry Hanson, vice president for construction and property management, eager to don their hard hats to give us a sneak preview. We met Considine and Hanson in the third-floor lobby of the old building at 281 Locust Street. We were issued Turner Construction Company hard hats and invited to follow them along familiar corridors to the door on the south (Exchange Street) side of the building that opened onto the construction site.

The third-floor atrium, in which kites and other aerial child-friendly art will be displayed as part of a community art program, was our first stop. It looks out on Perkins Square Park, which was being restored as we watched. A portion of the city park was taken for construction of the wing. In return, the hospital has replanted trees and shrubs, installed new lights and benches, and created a brick walk outlining the boundaries of the property given to the city by the Perkins family. In addition, Ronald McDonald Charities installed a playground. The hospital's child life department views the park as a place to help get the young patients back into their normal environments.

Inside, two fourth-floor balconies overlook the main lobby on the Exchange Street level of the atrium. One will be a waiting room for the day surgery department. The other will be a waiting room for the inpatient surgery department. Windows of patient rooms on the sixth, seventh, and eighth floors look out on the atrium.

The gift shop, operated by the hospital women's board, will be on the west (Locust Street) side of the lobby. Its entrance is shaped like the front of a small cottage. The lobby overlooks a smaller lower lobby on the second-floor east (Bowery Street) side of the hospital. This is the entrance most people will use. It has an automated revolving door large enough to accommodate people in wheelchairs and leads to elevators and an escalator to the main lobby, which runs alongside a wall decorated with giant-size versions of children's building blocks. A visitors' waiting room and a chapel will be off the main lobby. Another room will house a library that parents of patients may use.

We took the elevator to the eighth floor and began working our way downstairs.

The eighth floor will house adolescent and child psychiatry services, which has grown out of its space in the 1927 and 1947 sections of the hospital. The seventh floor has fifty-four single rooms for infants and toddlers. Each has a bed for the patient and a couch that opens to a bed for the parents. Some have sinks for the baby's bath. Some have showers for parents. Each room has its own special decor.

On the sixth floor, Chuck found his first drawing. Looking east along a corridor, he noticed that the perspective line continued beyond the building and corresponded perfectly with Buchtel Avenue. The sixth floor has forty-eight single rooms for adolescent and school-aged patients. The decor is tailored to the age group. Some sixth-floor patient rooms have windows looking out on a playground that has been created on the fifth-floor roof of an older section of the hospital. We walked onto that roof to find artificial turf with a built-in hopscotch course. The wall of the 1927 section of the hospital is to have a door installed and will soon feature a mural.

The fifth floor is filled with air-handling equipment for the floors above it and duct work and other special equipment for the operating rooms on the fourth floor. Placing the mechanical equipment on the fifth floor saved money and allowed for ceilings in the operating rooms to be higher, Hanson said.

The fourth floor will be the hospital's biggest. It will have eight new operating rooms, the smallest of which is larger than the largest in the old section. It also will have a new surgical recovery room, a pediatric intensive care unit, and two balcony waiting rooms. Hanson called the neonatal intensive care unit a place where miracles are performed. It will have fifty-nine beds, fifty-three in the new wing and six, for chronic cases, in the old.

We returned to the third floor, which the administrators described as the hospital's "Main Street," the major connector between the new and old buildings. The admitting department will be there and, eventually, the administrative offices, which have been located in a separate building on Locust Street for several years.

The second floor will be the first to be completed, Hanson said, and the first floor, housing the emergency department, will be the last. The emergency department will have three trauma rooms, which Hanson said will be like mini-operating rooms. The department will be prepared to handle sixty-four thousand patients a year.

We concluded our tour in the first-floor mechanical department, which, like the fifth-floor version, is filled with steam pipes and chillers for floors one through four, a big yellow generator to supply the hospital with emergency power, and a utility tunnel connecting the new power plant with the old.

While the construction crew completes its work, a hospital team of two hundred is preparing for the move, which will be completed over two days in May.

JULY 3, 1994

Looking through the Steel

Inventure Place, the $38 million home of the National Inventors Hall of Fame, was our destination, but we decided to approach it from the construction workers' perspective. The idea had been born a month earlier when we peered over the side of the Exchange Street bridge just east of Broadway to watch a large crane being unloaded and assembled by another crane next to the railroad tracks. The view north to University Avenue and the Inventure Place construction site was a study in activity only pedestrians would ever see. We were en route to College Street for the walk we described in the June 5 magazine. But we decided we had to return to share the sights of the construction staging area.

Stacks of blue insulation sheeting were piled high near the base of the Exchange Street bridge, where we started walking north along the dirt road that parallels the railroad tracks. Nearby, metal sections of scaffolding looked like pieces from a giant Tinker Toy set. The yellow Kelly Equipment Company crane we had seen in action a month earlier stood idle alongside the tracks. Stored along the tracks behind the old Erie passenger depot were stacks of wooden beams, posts and planks of various thicknesses, and piles of wooden pallets.

Just ahead, the dirt road forked. The left branch headed uphill toward the short stub of East Buchtel Avenue that runs between Broadway and the railroad valley. The right branch ran downhill to an area congested with workers' cars, construction vehicles, and more materials. As we pondered which way to go, a Lockhart Construction Company tractor lumbered up the ramp to pick up a trailer loaded with material for the site. We decided the lower road was no place for pedestrians and took to the high ground, noting along the way the 1947 cornerstone on the northeast corner of the Erie depot and noticing for the first time the parking meters on both sides of the East Buchtel stub.

As we approached Broadway, we ran smack into a study in lines and shadows—the Burger Structural Steel framework of the University of Akron's renovated Polsky parking deck. Seen from a car zipping along Broadway, the construction project is anything but impressive, just a steel skeleton that by the time you read this may be covered over with its new exterior finish. But viewed from across the street in the side yard of Akron's Old Stone Schoolhouse, it was a picture waiting to be made. And the picture improved with every step we took, as we studied familiar downtown Akron landmarks through the steel girders.

UA's William C. Jennings Plaza, at the southeast corner of Broadway and University Avenue, provided a good place from which to watch the activity at Inventure Place. The well-manicured plaza was a gift to the university from Jennings, a member of the UA class of 1962. It was neat as a pin and an inviting place to pause on a walk across campus or along Broadway. But we were the only visitors—no doubt because school was not in session. Studying the construction in progress across the street, we were hard pressed to guess what the finished building would look like. The curved steel framework appeared more decorative than functional, like a billowing sail on an old-time schooner. The activity on several levels on the other side of the steel lived up to the message of the banner that stretched across the front of the construction site: "Excitement is Being Built by the Inventure Place Team." And it provided the artist with his second subject.

Just below the bridge that carries University Avenue over the railroad valley, I spotted a lone worker sanding and buffing a stack of square metal plates. He wore jeans, a white apron over his bare chest, and a blue bandanna around his neck. A young black man with a shaved head, he could have come out of central casting for the role of the blacksmith in a Western movie. He worked steadily during the several minutes I watched, applying an electric sander and buffer to one plate at a time, then spraying each piece with a clear liquid we guessed to be kerosene and adding it to a stack of finished plates.

Inventure Place was under construction when we visited in 1994.

One of Akron's new bicycle-patrol police officers pedaled across the bridge as we prepared to cross University Avenue. Dressed in blue shorts, shirt, and helmet, he might have been taken at a glance for any other cyclist—except for the sidearm he carried.

From the north side of University Avenue, we could see that the construction staging area extended all the way to Quaker Square. We also noted that there is more to Inventure Place than appears on the surface. The lower portion of the building just may be more interesting than what can be seen from street level on Broadway. Square windows look out on the railroad valley, and a door large enough for a truck to pass through opens onto the road-way alongside the railroad tracks.

As we studied the site from across the tracks at the E. J. Thomas Hall plaza, the lunch whistle blew and workers began to pour out of the site. Most interesting of all was the exit of one hard-hatted fellow who emerged from a square window and climbed, monkeylike, down at least two stories of scaffolding to the ground.

SEPTEMBER 1, 1996

Walking the Girders

We didn't really walk the girders, but we touched a few and saw plenty of workers balancing on the high beams at construction and remodeling sites all over downtown Akron. Our half-day walking tour demonstrated once again that Akron is a work in progress. There were hard-hatted workers every-where we looked. We spotted the first four on the light tower over what will be the Main Street entrance of the new Canal Park stadium. We watched them scamper up and down the steel from a spot in the Key Bank and Evans Building parking lot on Maiden Lane Alley, just north of East Exchange Street. The Canal Park Tower on West State Street stood in the background, framed by one of the light tower's arches. The backs of the buildings along the north side of the alley were a study in contrasts, with ivy covering bricked-in windows and a rusted fire escape beside a black satellite dish on the roof, and the stadium's modern infield light tower in the background.

The skywalk connecting the new parking deck at Mill Street and Broad-way with the John S. Knight Center was our next stop. Along the way, we ad-mired the lush flowers, shrubs, and even two cornstalks along the sidewalk at the CitiCenter Parking Deck on South High Street and, across the street, the cross designs in the brickwork of both the High Street Christian Church and its neighbor, Zion Lutheran Church. We were reminded to "Trust Jesus" in white paint on a black metal utility pole.

Eight downtown construction sites show Akron as a work in progress.

Four workers—two on scaffolding and two on girders above them—cautiously helped a crane operator guide into place a section of steel about ten feet long and eight feet wide at the Knight Center end of the new skywalk. Then we watched as another worker began to weld the steel into place. The white brick corner of the Knight Center at Broadway and Mill, which I found so bland looking on our January visit, had improved, due to the addition of the skywalk's red brick entranceway and grand spiral staircase.

We watched two workers wearing hard hats and yellow climbing harnesses rise to the top of the parking deck in a construction elevator. When they got to the top, they began working on the grid for green-tinted panes that will match those at the Knight Center.

The walk to our next stop, the new First United Methodist Church of Akron at Mill Street near Union, revealed some hardhat sites we hadn't anticipated. From the bridge that carries Mill over the railroad tracks, we spotted two workers removing air ducts from the roof of the old REA Express building at Quaker Square. It was the start of demolition that will add to that complex's parking space. Beyond that scene, to the south, a crane lifted a big yellow bucket to workers on the roof of an attractive University of Akron building we have yet to see up close and identify. The bridge also offered a view of Inventure Place we had never noticed before. We discovered that road salt has taken its toll on the bridge's sidewalk, which was poured in 1959, according to the thirty-seven-year-old impression made by the contractor.

Bricklayers were adding exterior courses of red brick to the interior gray cinderblock walls when we arrived at the Methodist church site. The scaffolding they stood on resembled old biplanes flown in aviation's early days. Looking through the church's steel skeleton, we admired the 126-year-old International Order of Odd Fellows Temple, which we later learned is going to be renovated for use as a coffeehouse.

We hoofed it along Market Street to Main Street, pausing at Maiden Lane just long enough to admire two ornate styles of windows on the east-side wall of the Hermes Building, which has housed the Dettling Florist Shop since 1926.

Then we took our first close look at the Everett Building at the northeast corner of Market and Main. We had been following the progress of developer Anthony Troppe's renovation for months, waiting for just the right moment to do our fieldwork. Workers on scaffolding were painting the faux-stone exterior trim around and above the ground-level windows, which had been exposed for the first time since People's Federal acquired it in the 1970s. The Everett Building has five stories on the Market side and six on Main. Chuck's research turned up old photos showing the building before a fire in 1897. It then was three-and-a-half stories tall, with two towers facing Market, and it housed the Academy of Music. The building's signature iron balcony and large half-circle window on Market were there before and after the fire.

We were at the traffic island halfway across Main when Chuck found the vantage point from which to draw the construction site on the Federal Building plaza, where fenced-in plywood ramps led pedestrians to the building entrance on Market and long sections of granite from the wall of the plaza were numbered and crisscrossed like giant puzzle pieces.

As we zigzagged west on the State Street bridge en route to Cedar Street and our final destinations, the smell of mortar dust from the stadium site was in the air. Grading was underway on what will become the playing field.

We found a crane towering over the new Akron Metropolitan Housing Authority administration building on Cedar Street between Bowery and Locust streets. We had planned to conclude our walk at the former George Building at the northwest corner of Main and Exchange, but we were rewarded with a bonus on the way, a terrific view from the south side of the Cedar Street bridge over the Ohio & Erie Canal and the brand-new sidewalk the city of Akron had poured along the canal's east bank. The new walkway could be reached from a new flight of steps at the rear of the AES Building's parking lot. From the bridge's north side, Chuck captured a view of the George Building, which David Jacobs is converting into an office, retail, and entertainment complex. It was framed by the backs of buildings along Orleans Avenue, one of the most picturesque spots in town.

NOVEMBER 6, 1988

Going by Goodrich

The buildings on opposite sides of South Main Street at the southern edge of downtown Akron stand as monuments to change. Viewed from any angle, the sleek, modern structure housing the Uniroyal Goodrich corporate offices (in 2006, the home of Gojo Industries) seems to anchor downtown and draws the eye away from the older, red brick buildings that fill the block on the west side of Main, between Cedar and Bartges Streets. Until recently, there was little reason for anyone to walk this stretch of Main Street. Even when the complex housed the world headquarters and manufacturing operations of B. F. Goodrich, workers arrived by car, parking in the Opportunity Park Garage on South High Street, or by Metro bus. Lunchtime strollers constituted most of the pedestrian traffic.

But our collective curiosity was piqued a few weeks ago by the activity at the south end, where Stuart Lichter's Covington Capital Corporation attracted thirty-five thousand people for the opening of Canal Place Market. This isn't a story about what's inside the cavernous buildings at the Bartges end of the complex, but rather what we saw on our walk there and beyond.

Vacant buildings (not part of Canal Place) look worse up close. The Main Street door at the northeast corner of the complex is unlocked, open to any vandal or vagrant, in spite of the "Enter at your own risk" sign. A peek through the jagged glass of the many broken windows reveals acres of emptiness. Building permits dated 1984 and 1985 are posted at the entrance, along with warnings that hard hats are required. A rural-style mailbox anchored to a steel stand in the doorway lists the names P. J. Neman, M. Pedone Construction Company, Builders Management, and Main Exchange (the former occupants). A phone number posted at the entrance has been changed to an unpublished number, we later learn. It is a discouraging beginning, enough to cause the less than optimistic to turn around.

The sight of people ahead on the sidewalk improves the landscape. It is

An iron gate symbolized the adaptive reuse of the former B. F. Goodrich complex.

4:30 P.M., quitting time, and employees begin to pour out of buildings on both sides of Main Street. They can also be seen moving along the two-level skywalk that connects the Uniroyal Goodrich building with the former B. F. Goodrich plant. Parked at a meter on the east side of Main, a black Cadillac, circa 1940, attracts admiring glances of passersby.

Across the street, in the shadow of the skywalk, a miniature barber pole spins in an office window, and for the first time we notice an old barbershop sign on one of the old complex's many entrances. Barber Frank Gartner is alone in his two-chair shop. He has been a barber in downtown Akron since 1950, first at Buchtel and Main, then at the B. F. Goodrich World Headquarters, where he kept three chairs filled. He moved across the street when Uniroyal Goodrich took over the building. Canal Place is his new landlord. Gartner maintains his ties with B. F. Goodrich by operating a one-chair shop at its Crystal Lake headquarters in Bath.

There is a big-city, canyonlike feel to this stretch of Main Street, unlike anything we've experienced downtown. Perhaps a better way to state it is that this doesn't look or feel like Akron. The parklike front and back sections of Uniroyal Goodrich, with its many flags flapping in the breeze, and the bustle of pedestrian traffic, short though it is, create a mood that disappears when we've walked just a short distance beyond.

The green iron fence that stretches the length of the old complex, on the other hand, when viewed against the background of red brick and dark, empty windows, brings us back to reality. It is the day before Canal Place Market is to open and property manager Dennis K. Oleksuk is concluding a conversation with a visitor at the entrance, where cement finishers are still at work. It is still called the Jackson Street Gate, named for the city street that once ran south off Main. Ornamental gates and a red brick walkway will be added later, Oleksuk promises.

We're now at Bartges, a wide thoroughfare with trees planted in the divider strip. To the west, the old complex stretches for another long block. Across the street is a residential neighborhood, the Dorothy O. Jackson Terrace, and beyond it a park. We knew that. We've driven past many times before. But it suddenly becomes real when you're standing there, really seeing peoples' homes, their backyards, their bicycles, and baby buggies. From the park, which is bisected by the Ohio & Erie Canal, downtown is a distant reality somewhere beyond the complex still affectionately called "the Goodrich" by many.

JULY 2, 1989

Strolling Along Summit

The brilliant green ivy first caught my eye as I waited to make a left turn onto East Market Street from Summit Street weeks before we decided to walk that short block between Market and East Mill. Ivy covers most of three sides of the old frame house, including its top-floor dormer, a portion of its roof, and even the television antenna; it looks like something out of a Stephen King story. The home, its well-ventilated garage, and another frame house on South Broadway, viewed against Akron's downtown skyline, reminded me of a children's story, read long ago, about a city that grew up around the home of an owner reluctant to make way for progress and the wrecker's ball.

Chuck, who had never noticed either house before, agreed the scene begged to be drawn. But from which perspective? We started around the block to find out. The view from Broadway was good for a drawing. A lilac bush and English ivy grow in front of the home on Broadway, which has three mailboxes, a "Beware of Dog" sign, a homemade wooden fire escape, and a sign that once electrically heralded the house as headquarters of a real estate investment firm. But the artist liked the view from Summit better and decided to retrace his steps to draw from his original vantage point while the writer continued around the block.

Broadway between Market and Mill is a street of parking lots, not all of them filled or, in a few instances, even used. Blue and white Perrier umbrellas shaded people sitting at tables in the courtyard at Quaker Square, giving the

The ivy-covered home and garage on Summit Street were razed soon after our visit.

southeast corner of Broadway and Mill a continental flair. A real treat appeared around the corner at Court Yard Square, the restored ninety-one-year-old building at the northeast corner of Mill and Summit. I had zipped past it countless times since a *Beacon Magazine* story chronicled its restoration in 1986, but I never realized what a stately jewel it was until I stood on the sidewalk, staring at its new cornerstone.

Back at our starting point in front of the ivy-covered home, Chuck offered a peek at his sketchbook. Then we watched as, one by one, seven school buses drew up to the curb outside Weaver Industries' Akron Training Center at the southeast corner of Summit and Market. We counted twenty-six lion heads and six likenesses of Mercury staring down from the roof line of the building, which once was home to the *Beacon Journal* and later was the Akron Public Library, before it moved to South Main and became the Akron-Summit County Public Library. Then it was back-to-work time for us, but not before we paid a visit to the place with the continental flair.

(A postscript: The ivy-covered home and its well-ventilated garage fell to progress and the wrecker's ball to make way for more parking soon after this story was published.)

MAY 11, 1997

Night Lights

Charles F. Brush caused quite a stir when he illuminated Cleveland's Public Square with twelve electric arc lights in 1879. I got an idea of what it might have been like to witness that historic scene a few weeks ago when I was leaving work after dark. As I drove down the ramps of the newspaper's parking deck, I noticed that the north wall of windows at the former B. F. Goodrich World Headquarters on South Main Street were ablaze with light.

It was a view of the building I'd seen countless times before—except for the intensity of the white light that appeared to be coming from inside the building. It wasn't, of course. I soon realized that I was seeing one of the banks of lights at Canal Park reflected in the windows. Quite literally, I was

Lights at Canal Park set Akron aglow.

seeing Akron in a new light. It offered another excuse for Chuck and me to mosey on over to the stadium. But this time, we stayed outside, walking around downtown Akron on a Friday night when the Aeros were playing at home, and soaking up new images of light and shadow created by the stadium lights.

We started by watching the sunset from the roof of the University of Akron's Polsky parking garage. Two UA police officers shared the view with us. The sun was sinking slowly over a low bank of clouds, so we had a few minutes to enjoy the bird's-eye look at the busy street scene as quite a few people parked in lots east of Main and walked along High Street and Buchtel Avenue toward the stadium. The game was already in progress, and we could hear the crowd and the public-address announcements and could read part of the scoreboard.

At 8:05 P.M., the sun began to cut through the cloudbank just to the left of the steel arches above the stadium's main entrance. By 8:10 P.M., the sun was all but down, its curve just visible behind the treeline on the horizon. A minute later, it was gone, but its glow filled the area where it had been. We marveled at the contrast between that warm, golden light and the cold, man-made lights at the stadium, which also reflected back at us from the windows of Children's Hospital. The temperature began to drop as soon as the sun disappeared. It got dark quickly, but in a way that was different from all the other times we had walked this way.

We were far from alone on the sidewalk, and we wondered aloud when we last saw families with small children walking downtown on a Friday night. The city was alive with people, many arriving late for the baseball game, or leaving early, or lining up to get into Vault 328, a new Main Street bistro.

Standing in front of a boarded-up building at the southwest corner of Main and Exchange Streets, we observed that the fronts of the Evans and Kaiser buildings across Main were bathed in stadium light as if it were daytime. So was the west wall of the former A. C. & Y. Building at 12 East Exchange, though its front stood in the Evans Building's shadow.

Moving west along Exchange, we paused to look south along Orleans Avenue and noted that the blue light of the stadium's scoreboard was reflected in the windows on the north wall of the Advanced Elastomer Systems building at Main and Cedar Streets. Taking a 180-degree look at the sky, we noted how its color darkened from blue-gray in the west to almost black in the east.

From the Exchange Street bridge over the Ohio & Erie Canal, we had a great view of Water Street, where the buildings were also bathed in stadium light and that of the streetlights installed as part of the Canal Park project. More colorful scoreboard reflections made the windows of one building look like a giant TV screen. As we approached Water and Exchange Streets, Chuck spotted the Hale-Bopp comet in the western sky, its fuzzy tail a nighttime version of the jet trails that have become emblematic of our daytime walks.

Chuck found a vantage point he liked at the Bowery Street entrance of Children's Hospital, where the stadium lights reflected off the sides of the Canal Square building at 80 West Center Street, the O'Neil's building, Canal Park Tower Apartments at 50 West State Street, and the top floors of the Mayflower Manor.

The Aeros game was winding down, and some fans were already on the move for the exits. But some stayed to the end, including a man who was watching the action from a fourth-floor window of the Canal Park Tower and three young men who watched from a picnic table on the elevated patio inside the ballpark on the left-field side. The three hopped the fence after the final out and joined the pedestrian parade that fanned out in every direction.

The stadium lights began to go off as we walked back toward the car, which was parked on Broadway at Buchtel. As they did, downtown Akron began to take on the look we remembered from before the ballpark was built. The memory wasn't bad, but the new look was better.

CHAPTER THREE

Akron's Skyline from All the Right Angles

The Goodyear blimp was just one of several recurring visual treats Chuck and I experienced during our years of hoofing it around the area. Such was the case in 1990, when the unmistakable drone of the blimp's engines was the climax of our visit to the Akron Zoo. Jet trails and the Akron skyline were among the other indelible images we shared with readers through the 1990s and into the new century.

JULY 1, 1990

At the Zoo

Wimpy, a barn owl, stared blankly at us from a portable cage as we sauntered in from the parking lot. Volunteer "edzoocator" Pam Moore was taking Wimpy on a field trip to Seiberling Elementary School, which, it seemed by the end of the morning, was the only school in the area that wasn't sending students on a field trip to the zoo. Hefty, Wimpy's mate, was staying behind to be stared at by throngs of children, whose yellow buses were beginning to arrive.

The zoo is quiet before 10 A.M., its opening time from mid-April to mid-October. Most of the squirrel monkeys were still asleep when we passed their exhibit. The quiet ended at the stroke of 10, when a happy swarm of youthful humanity began its visit. Shouts of "Cowabunga!" proliferated, and one was struck by the way all the boys seemed to resemble Bart Simpson. The hum of saws and the pounding of hammers were music to the ears of zoo staffers as work progressed on the expansion of the zoo administration building, one of several projects going on.

Workmen were adding a second floor to the east end of the building, which began as a WPA-built city of Akron parks maintenance building in the 1930s. The building housed the Akron Museum of Natural History for about twenty years. As the zoo grew, it gave exhibits to the University of Akron, and offices were set up in the building. Eventually, visitors will be able to sit on benches in the B. F. Goodrich recycle garden, a new rest area near the administration building. The benches and picnic tables in a pavilion just up the hill are made from recycled "plastic wood." Recycled vinyl mats cover the ground in the high-traffic rest area.

But we didn't come to sit on benches. We came to look at Akron from the high ground, just as Colonel Simon Perkins did when he selected the site for his stone mansion a mile or so north of the zoo. From the highest level on the zoo's west side, near Perkins Park Drive, most of downtown can be seen easily, even through the trees. It's an even better view when the trees are bare, and best of all at night during the Christmas season, when the zoo is ablaze with colored lights. The Akron that Perkins looked down at was a village just beginning, with one- and two-story buildings along a new canal. Today's view is of buildings ten times that height.

Our vantage point, overlooking the cage of Coffee and Kareem Abdul Jaguar, was near the noisiest place in the zoo, the nesting quarters of a pair of trumpeter swans. The youngsters were drawn by the incessant honking of one black-billed swan, which came to the split-rail fence to inspect the inspectors. As if trained to do so, the kids honked in unison until the din was maddening. Then, as suddenly as it started, the noise stopped as, one by one, the crowd

The Goodyear blimp highlighted our visit to the Akron Zoo.

began looking skyward at the Goodyear blimp, which slowly droned into view. No one said it, but the silence and the wonder on the young faces reflected the mood. It was truly awesome.

Sky Walk

The sky above downtown Akron was streaked with sunlight and criss-crossed with jet trails that demanded to be preserved on film or canvas. But we had to move quickly, before the winds erased the picture. That view—from the top of the hill at South Portage Path and Copley Road—sent us on a circuitous journey in which we discovered something new about two of Akron's oldest streets. Our walk—and ride—took us from the Summit County Historical Society's Perkins Stone Mansion, where Chuck captured his skyline illustration, to a forgotten stub of Locust Street that neither of us knew existed until we stumbled upon it.

It all happened by chance. We had planned to walk around a residential neighborhood in South Akron, but the heavy jet traffic sent us searching for the best place from which to view the air show. Such spontaneity required a slight change of rationale. Our assignment, which began eleven years ago this month, was open-ended and remains so today: Show and tell the readers what we see when we park our cars and take a walk. The only other time a car had been part of the equation—beyond transporting us to the start of a walk—was in 1995, when we explored sections of the Ohio & Erie Canal towpath wherever we could find them between Akron and Bolivar. This was a bit different—more like that scene in *Raiders of the Lost Ark* in which someone asks Indiana Jones what he's going to do to get the religious artifact back from the bad guys, and he replies, "I don't know. I'm making this up as I go along."

We went to Perkins Mansion because the high ground on which it is built is a great place from which to view downtown Akron's skyline. Once there, we wondered whether the mansion would look as good from downtown—if

Jet vapor trails over Perkins Hill.

it could be seen at all. Chuck knew just the spot from which we could find out, the roof of the parking deck at Children's Hospital.

But first we drove down Copley and Cedar, stopping briefly at Bell Street to see if the mansion was visible from there. It wasn't, but we did observe, standing on a grass and concrete remnant of what had been the foundation of a home, how the neighborhood landscape had been forever altered by the extension of Cedar in 1976, when West Exchange Street was made one way between South Main Street and Rhodes Avenue. Chuck recalled living on Five Points Drive, part of which was vacated for the Cedar extension, from the second grade through part of the fifth. The family home was so close to Grace School that he could hear the school bell ring from his living room, signaling the time to run to class. Cedar now runs where his house stood.

Our next stop was a parking meter on the side street that runs along the south side of the parking deck across Locust from Children's Hospital. The side street is the westernmost stub of Buchtel Avenue—a fact we had forgotten, if we ever knew it. Buchtel and Locust were among the streets on the original plat for Akron, although all the streets on the plat were unnamed except for Buchtel, which was then called Middlebury. That's because it was the road from the village of Middlebury to the canal town being planned in 1825 by General Simon Perkins and Paul Williams. The street was renamed on March 4, 1889. Expansions of the University of Akron and Children's Hospital, construction of Canal Park, and creation of the Buchtel Common have left Buchtel Avenue in four unconnected sections.

We walked to Dart Street at the western end of Buchtel and peered across the innerbelt at the neighborhood that borders Glendale Cemetery, and wondered about the "For Sale" sign posted on a chain link fence that seemed to be the cemetery's. From this vantage point, we couldn't see Perkins Mansion or much else through the trees on the horizon.

The roof of the parking deck provided much better viewing. Immediately below us were the hospital's helicopter pad and a stately old tree, which Chuck had included in an earlier illustration. Missing from the view now was the residential setting, an occupied home and backyard in which the tree then stood.

Today the tree stands in a hospital parking lot. The panorama from south to north was breathtaking. We recognized the white columns of Perkins Mansion through the trees, and, for good measure, we picked out many of the places in the city we had visited in earlier walks.

We could have ended the story there, but we wanted to find out what was for sale on the other side of the innerbelt. So we drove west across the innerbelt to Rand Street and then wove our way through the tiny neighborhood on the hill, along streets named Wills, Dawes, King, and Oak Park. We counted no fewer than ten U.S. flags flying from front porches, and it wasn't even a holiday!

Our last stop was at the chain-link fence we had seen from the hospital. A discarded tire occupied the middle of the brick-paved street that ended at the fence, overgrown with vines. The fence ran along the western rim of the high ground above the innerbelt, and was adjacent to, but not part of, the cemetery. We parked the car and surveyed the surroundings. This was a section of Locust forgotten by all except those who live in the neighborhood. Remnants of driveways and foundations marked the places where homes had stood on one side of the street. And on the other side was a parking lot that had been used until recently by hospital employees. The sign for its sale is what we had seen earlier. A sidewalk to nowhere ran along the outside of the fence, and a footpath worn into the grassy hillside led down to Rand and the bridge to the hospital.

The view of downtown lacked the drama of the one that had started the day, but it was spectacular, thanks to the midday sun, which cast deep shadows on the city's tallest buildings.

JULY 5, 1992

Angles and Arches

As luck would have it, the headline and the concept for this story occurred to us six months and eighty degrees ago, on a morning when the wind-chill

Akron street is a study in angles and arches.

factor was twelve below zero and we were preparing an article for the February 2 magazine. We were standing on the second floor of the new University of Akron College of Business Administration building on Broadway, allowing the circulation to return to our fingers, when we noticed through the front windows the repetition of shapes in the architecture all around us.

St. Bernard's Catholic Church, a product of the nineteenth century, loomed across the street, the angles of its roofline and spires repeated in the lines of the new skybridge linking the Business Administration Building with the former Polsky's garage at Broadway and State Street. But that was just the beginning.

Looking west along State, we had a clear vista for five blocks, all the way to Children's Hospital. It included the roofline angles and window arches of both Grace United Church of Christ at 172 West Bowery Street and the YMCA at 80 West Center Street. To our right, the angles and arches of other buildings along Broadway drew our attention as if they were outlined in neon. Buildings bearing no resemblance to each other were suddenly linked by these geometric shapes. Sure, a geometry teacher might argue that the angles weren't all exactly the same. But that didn't matter. It was the aesthetic impression that counted.

We couldn't explore the subject further. We were, after all, on another assignment. So we decided to let time be the judge. We would return later to see whether the angles and arches were as impressive on second examination. It took six months to get back to that same vantage point. We were not disappointed.

The arched windows of the Summit County Courthouse annex and those of St. Bernard's and its former school building might have been drawn by the same hand. Could these have influenced the architect who designed the arches atop the modern Ocasek Government Office Building or the designer who decided to paint windowlike brown arches on the silos at the Hilton at Quaker Square? We wondered.

It got to be a game of who could spot "new" angles or arches as we walked north along Broadway. We counted six stone window arches on the back wall of Zion Lutheran Church, which fronts on South High Street at Bowery. Their design was the same as those on the courthouse, its annex, and St. Bernard's.

The vista south on Broadway from the entrance of the Morley Health Center is almost as dramatic as the view to the north. From that spot, the roofline of the CitiCenter duplicates the angled shape of the tower of St. Mary's Catholic Church eight blocks away at South Main Street and Thornton Avenue. And we were not surprised to note that windows along the top of the CitiCenter are arched. The skeleton of the new skybridge that links the Morley building with the Ocasek building contains twenty angled arches.

We paused on the way back along Broadway to do a detailed inventory of St. Bernard's and its former school, for the proliferation of arches at these buildings was what first caught our eyes. Twin spires looking like upended sugar cones atop red brick columns flank the school building's arched entrance. Above the front door are two arched windows, and above them an arched stone niche containing a statue I had never noticed before. Except for the arches, the brick school building bears no resemblance to the stone church, whose texture begs to be touched.

St. Bernard's towers stand as tall as two ten-story buildings. The slate at the top of the northern spire is loose, and we wondered about how repairs might be made on so steep-angled a surface. Pigeons flew in and out of portals above the arched belfries, from which the bells appeared to be absent. A loudspeaker in the northern belfry was all that was visible from our vantage point below.

We counted eighteen arches—windows and niches—on the Broadway side of each tower. Add to that sixteen more arches above three arched doors, and you've got fifty-five arches on the front of the building. We stopped counting there, wondering if anyone else would find this as interesting as we did. Perhaps, as they say, you had to be there.

The vapor trail of a high-flying plane caught Chuck's eye when we were nearing Broadway and East Exchange Street. As we laughed about this link to some of the previous stories in this series, we heard the unmistakable drone of the Goodyear blimp, which came into view in the southeastern sky. It would be too much to hope for a train, Chuck said, just before a Chessie engine rolled north along the tracks paralleling Broadway, pulling a long line of identical cars bearing the Coke Express logo. It was while we were pondering these links to previous pedestrian adventures that he noticed the roof of the old Erie Railroad station at Broadway and Exchange, giving us one more angle for our story.

JANUARY 7, 1996

An Akron Overlook that Most of Us Overlook

It's a fact: A ballpoint pen is likely to fail in freezing weather or when the writing surface is wet from falling snow. I relearned this lesson on a visit to Waters Park at the north end of the All-America Bridge in Akron's North Hill neighborhood. I'd brought a pencil to write with, so the minor annoyance was more than made up for by the wintry view of downtown Akron and the Little Cuyahoga River valley through the naked trees. We came for the view, which these same trees in full bloom hide behind a curtain of green most of the time the park is in use.

Waters is small as parks go, a grassy haven on the bluff at North Main and Olive Streets, across from Summa Health System's St. Thomas Hospital. It has benches, a few picnic tables, and ten shuffleboard courts enclosed by a chain-link fence, against which a harvest of fallen leaves was trapped before the season's first snow. We had concluded a *Beacon Magazine* feature about the bridge at the southeast corner of the park with the intention of returning when the leaves were gone. It took us seven years, but the view was worth the wait.

More impressive than the downtown skyline is the valley, which is lined with streets and has more homes than many small towns. The neighborhood below the bluff intrigued us, so we hiked down a wide, winding drive that ended at Glenwood Avenue. We had never noticed the drive before, but it

Waters Park overlooks downtown Akron.

apparently was a second entrance to the park or, perhaps, the original entrance. The drive is bordered by stone walls that are low—perhaps three feet high—for most of its length but which rise to at least six feet at the bottom of the hill and end at two large stone gate posts. A thick, rusty chain stretches between the posts, an indication that the entrance hasn't been open to cars lately.

We walked east on Glenwood to the first intersection, where Oak Street runs south a short way and then bends east along a second bluff, and Butler Avenue runs north, all uphill. The area reminded us of neighborhoods in Pittsburgh, with houses built in terraces because of the terrain. It's an old but well-kept neighborhood, full of homes that bear many signs of the sweat equity their owners have poured into them. After rounding the bend on Oak, we doubled back and trudged through the snow up Butler and back to Olive and the park, which we now viewed in the context of the neighborhood it serves.

A plaque on a large boulder identifies the park as a gift to the city of Akron in 1934 from Frank Hugh Waters in memory of his wife, Cora Swift Waters, and their daughter, Mary Waters Sneddon. The same boulder bears a faded red spray paint pledge of undying love, "Joey + Kathy." Nearby, an old concrete lamppost stands idle, stained from years of rust that has drained down from its metal frame.

The park has a terraced stone section that looks like an amphitheater but doesn't appear to have seen much use lately. Covered with snow, it had the appearance of an ancient ruin. Just south of that, below the wide drive and perched on the edge of the bluff, was a small stone overlook that looks older than sixty years. It is likely the overlook was built by Waters. We learned from old newspaper clippings that he was a lawyer with the firm of Roetzel & Andress. Waters came to Akron shortly after he was graduated from Yale Law School in 1887 and married Cora Swift in 1892. They lived near Glendale Cemetery until they discovered the view from the bluff on North Hill and built their home there.

The story would have ended here except for a phone call from a librarian who helped in our research. Stow librarian Christine Caccamo had to share a story she's heard since she was a child about "the mean man" who lived in the Waters mansion. Her father, Ernest Caccamo, grew up on North Hill. When he was about seven years old, he climbed over the wall at what was then the Waters residence and picked some berries. The butler caught him, gave him a thrashing, then took him inside to his employer, who lectured him about stealing. The mansion is long gone and remembered by few, but Frank Waters decided to share the view with the community at his death in 1934.

JUNE 11, 2000

Frame of Reference

Nordberg LT105 stood its ground, looking Spielbergesque, a cross between a winged dinosaur and a futuristic transport suitable for travel in space and/or some remote desert. Nordberg LT105 is a black-and-white, tank-treaded, long-necked piece of earthmoving equipment, and its ground is the rubble and twisted metal of the demolition site between the Spaghetti Warehouse and the Ohio & Erie Canal, just a stone's—or, more appropriately—brick's throw from the spot where Dr. Benjamin Franklin Goodrich opened his rubber factory on the southern edge of Akron in 1870.

Akron was just forty-five years old and had been a city only five years when the B. F. Goodrich company opened for business on the canal near Falor Street. Today, as the city prepares to celebrate its centeseptequinary (that's a fancy way of saying 175th anniversary of its founding), Falor is an alley within the maze of buildings that comprise Canal Place.

All that remained of one of those buildings when we visited the site was its steel skeleton. We parked in the visitors' section of Lot No. 30 behind Canal Place Building No. 25, where the picturesque skywalk, one of the city's oldest, was sacrificed because it connected to the building being razed. A yellow guardrail ran along the west end of the lot. Beyond and below the rail, we could see the remnants of a brick wall and concrete floor of a long-forgotten subterranean room in the Goodrich complex.

A chain-link fence separated the lot and Canal Place from the construction site, where Nordberg LT150 and a few big yellow CATs—as in Caterpillar shovels—stood waiting to be used, and a couple of big rusty clawlike buckets sat in the dirt, waiting to be attached to shovels.

The steel girders formed a grid through which we could see the Cedar Street bridge, Canal Park, and the downtown skyline. It was this view that attracted us, because it represents the ongoing evolution of Akron, a city that keeps reinventing itself. When the demolition is completed, the city of Akron will begin work to provide additional parking for Advanced Elastomer Systems, in the former B. F. Goodrich buildings to the north; Gojo Industries, in the building erected in the 1970s as the Goodrich world headquarters; and Canal Place, which occupies the former Goodrich properties to the south.

The view through the steel focused on the former O'Neil's department store, another example of adaptive reuse of real estate, what with the cutting in half of the building in its renovation to become headquarters for the law firm of Roetzel & Andress.

The Spaghetti Warehouse will be in a freestanding building when the demolition is completed, and we'll all have a clear view of the canal from Main Street, Canal Place publicist Alice Hall told me after our visit. Hall also said twenty-one hundred people are employed in 130 businesses at Canal Place, which began its adaptive reuse of the Goodrich properties with the Covington Capital Corporation's purchase of twenty-nine buildings in 1988.

We drove to Canal Place Lot 31, just north of the demolition site, in search of other vantage points. We walked to the end of the wide sidewalk that runs along the canal behind the Advanced Elastomer Systems building and found the view to the north—with the downtown buildings reflected in the canal and Old Glory flying from a staff in the AES parking lot—suitable for a chamber of commerce photo. The view to the south was of grass growing behind the paved Lot 31 and the canal, a promise of what is to come. In the end, Chuck chose to use the view through the steel girder grid because it captured something that was before it disappeared.

CHAPTER FOUR

Discovering Akron's Neighborhoods

From the humblest to the most upscale, Akron is a city of neighborhoods marked by community pride expressed in many ways. During our travels, Chuck Ayers and I visited virtually every corner of the city and came away with a treasure trove of historical footnotes and at least one urban legend.

SEPTEMBER 6, 1998

Upscale Area Surrounded by Splendor

We followed a yellow-brick road to get to the wide, two-lane, red-brick road named Mayfield Avenue in West Akron. Mayfield, with its mix of styles, among them Tudor, Georgian, Neo-Classical, and Italian Renaissance, defines the term "upscale." It has since the street was laid out at the turn of the twentieth century, we learned as we prepared for a preview of the site (eight homes and one garden) of the 1998 Progress Through Preservation Historic House Tour. We decided to examine the two-block Mayfield Allotment in the context of the larger neighborhood of which it is a part.

Grass was growing between the yellow-brick pavement of Everett Avenue, which runs south of West Market Street through the neighborhood where Chuck lives and has his studio. We walked the length of Everett, from Ardmore Avenue north to South Rose Boulevard to the tiny triangle that encompasses the city's Shady Park.

Along the way, we passed a white home trimmed in yellow, the onetime home of Dr. Robert H. Smith, who founded Alcoholics Anonymous in Akron, in 1935, with New York stockbroker William G. Wilson. A stone inscription at the home, now a museum, commemorates the work of the men known for years only as Dr. Bob and Bill W.

Farther up the street, we wondered who had decorated the bases of two utility poles with flowers. One pole also displayed black-eyed Susans in virtually every crack to a height of four feet. Retired University of Akron English professor Jim Switzer came walking by and guessed—correctly, we would learn—that nine-year-old Maia Kavooras, daughter of his neighbor, Molly Sullivan, had "planted" the flowers. Maia, who emerged from her home as we spoke, acknowledged her handiwork with a shy grin.

At Shady Park, we had a good view of Mayfield across Market Street. The southern entrance is marked by three stone columns, including one at the southern end of the traffic island that divides Mayfield. We crossed Market and walked the long block to Twin Oaks Road along the east side of Mayfield, where, we noted from the markings, new sidewalks had been poured in 1993. Gargoyles competed with lions as ornamental sculpture on display, and floral plantings along the traffic island rivaled those in many front yards.

Mayfield's homes bear out Akron architectural historian James A. Pahlau's description, written for the tour brochure. Pahlau said the allotment was laid out in 1900–01 "as Akron's continuing growth was demanding the development of upscale neighborhoods farther out West Hill." The stone columns—Pahlau called them piers—date to the beginning, as does the brick pavement, although the bricks were later covered by asphalt and remained so until neighborhood lobbying succeeded in having them uncovered in 1992. Mayfield predates Twin Oaks, which was built in 1907 after the Portage

The north end of Mayfield Avenue showcases Keep Akron Beautiful's loving care.

Country Club was established, and is not part of the Mayfield Allotment, he said.

Three homes were built by 1902. The count climbed to fifteen by 1910, thirty by 1915 (the year Stan Hywet Hall was built a few blocks away on Portage Path), and forty by 1926. Between 1913 and 1922, three homes were razed to make room for more expensive homes, Pahlau said. No more were built until a brick bungalow went up in 1949.

Chuck found the perspective for his illustration when we reached Twin Oaks and looked south along Mayfield. Market Street traffic was visible in the distance. In the foreground was a colorful display of roses, black-eyed Susans, and ground cover planted at the north end of the traffic island, a sign informed us, by Keep Akron Beautiful and the Mayfield Allotment Association.

We started back along the west side of the street, then took a detour west along Maplewood Avenue, which intersects in the middle of the Mayfield block. The L-shaped Maplewood, we learned from Pahlau's thumbnail sketch, was originally two streets. The section running west off Mayfield originally was named Vernon Avenue and was renamed after Maplewood was built parallel to Mayfield in 1910. Back at Market, we ended our walk by heading east along the sidewalk, which detours near the Mayfield intersection around an old oak we guessed to be three-and-one-half feet in diameter.

JANUARY 5, 1997

Triangulating a Square

Do you know the way to Highland Square? A songwriter could set that to music but probably couldn't answer the question. Look at the map of Akron. Highland Square doesn't show up. But the triangle formed by Highland Avenue, West Market Street and South Portage Path really jumps out at you. All of this is by way of introduction to our walk along sides of that triangle. It was familiar territory for me and moreso for Chuck, whose studio looks out on

Portage Path and the Akron elementary school named for it. As usual, there was much to be discovered in the most familiar places.

We had walked this stretch of Portage Path before in 1995, on our way back from Shady Park—another triangle, bounded by West Market, South Rose Boulevard, and Metlin Avenue—but our attention had then been focused on the terraced grounds of the Colony apartment complex on the west side of the street. This time we concentrated on the school. I've driven by and admired the Indian's profile on the school's addition many times but didn't know until Chuck told me that it was the work of artist Don Drumm (done in 1973 with chisel and sandblasting equipment). The real discoveries—easily missed by the motorist—were the three much older sculpted Indian heads above the school entrances on Portage Path. We also noted the school is still a Civil Defense fallout shelter, and counted sixteen windows that had been bricked in.

The empty building at the Portage Path and Market point of the triangle still displayed Clinton-Gore signs in the windows, along with a few other posters form the November elections and a sign advising all who read it of the new location of the insurance agency that had been housed there. A drive-through window on the building's east side recalled the days when a bank had a branch there.

We admired the rhododendron along the sidewalk bordering Walgreen's —once the site of Trolley Stop, née Brown Derby, née Yanko's. We also noted the absence of sidewalks leading to the building. Pedestrians get to dodge cars in the parking lot, and vice versa, just like your favorite shopping mall. But Highland Square isn't a shopping mall. It's an urban village where the villagers still walk to the shops, restaurants, library branch, and other destinations.

Around the corner on Market, our eyes were drawn to a sign on the side of Highland Theatre. A giant hand with the index finger extended literally pointed to Bob Ferguson's shoe repair shop, which occupies a tiny spot on the west side of the theater entrance. Chuck knows Ferguson, so we dropped in and ran into *Beacon Journal* photographer Phil Masturzo and copy editor Jim

Kavanagh. Masturzo was shooting pictures (for a feature story). Kavanagh was picking up some old shoes made new.

The Highland Theatre was being spruced up for its grand reopening December 26, so we weren't surprised to find the doors open. We were greeted by two employees of Ted Bare Enterprises, owners of the fifty-eight-year-old building. R. J. "Sonny" Bare, the owner's son, and Eric Johnson were moving furniture but took time out to turn on the house lights and show us around. It was my first peek, and Chuck hadn't been inside for several years.

Chuck chose an unusual view of the theater for his illustration when we rounded the corner from Market to Highland—the dead-end alley that runs behind the shops on Market to the side of the theater. While he was studying the backs of the shops for the right vantage from which to show the tangle of power lines, parked cars, porches, gutters, and downspouts, a car pulled up and an old acquaintance, Tom Murdock, board chairman of the M. F. Murdock Company, got out to ask directions to Angel Falls, the neighborhood's new coffee shop. We pointed him around the corner, then adjourned to another Highland Square eatery, Mary Coyle's, where we ran into another acquaintance, Becky Considine, who dropped in to buy chocolates for the holidays. We eschewed the candy and ice cream but couldn't pass up the ravioli.

JUNE 7, 1992

Touring a Firestone Legacy

We had new sidewalks to walk on during our special preview of the eighth annual Progress Through Preservation house tour June 28 in Akron's Firestone Park neighborhood. This will be the first time the tour has moved across town from the West Side, and Progress Through Preservation member Sylvia Johnson was obviously delighted as she showed us around the neighborhood she has called home since age three.

Some of the sidewalks being replaced along Firestone Park Boulevard and

Firestone Park School anchors the surrounding neighborhood.

its intersecting streets date to the establishment of the residential district. Harvey S. Firestone bought one thousand acres southeast of his factory in 1915 and hired landscape architect Alling De Forest to design a neighborhood around a park that was shaped like a shield, the company emblem. The Coventry Land and Improvement Company was organized to develop housing on six hundred acres bounded by East Archwood Avenue, Main and Brown Streets, and East Wilbeth Road. In October 1916, the park opened, and home sites were offered for sale to Firestone employees. First-day sales totaled 177, Johnson said.

We started our walk at the castle-tower entrance of Firestone Park School at the park's east end. The school opened in 1917 and housed grades kindergarten through eight until 1954, when the junior-high grades were moved out. Johnson was in Firestone Park's last eighth-grade class. The front of the school faces the park's shelter house, which was built by WPA workers during the Great Depression. Girard Avenue separated school and park property until a portion of the street was vacated, closed to motor vehicles, and turned into a wide walkway.

Chuck and I saw only the outside of eleven of the twelve homes on the tour, and we didn't have the guidebook tour participants will receive. But our guide's personal perspective and an invitation inside one home more than made up for any disappointment we might have felt. We walked the route she took to school, past the homes of her piano teacher and her childhood best friend. We got to see the house just off the boulevard where Johnson lived until she was married, and the first home she and her husband, Howard, purchased. We admired through her description a Tudor-style home, which has kitchen cupboards fashioned from the wood of old oak church pews by the home's second owner, a former industrial arts teacher.

"That's adaptive reuse to the max," said Johnson, who knows a bit about the subject through her work as director of the University of Akron's Hower House.

The tour features other Tudor-style homes, several Dutch colonials, and a few that were cut, packaged, and shipped for assembly by Sears years before the term "prefabricated" was coined. Johnson told us of "to-die-for" oak woodwork in one Tudor, "mint-condition" original oak woodwork in a bungalow, and oak ceiling beams and double French doors in a third home.

The icing on the cake came when we were invited inside a large colonial built on the eve of the Depression. After touring upstairs and down, we were treated to a cool drink and a look at the blueprints, which the original owners kept and passed along when the home was sold.

We walked back to the school, where we met principal Lynda Grieves and her husband, Bill. They are Progress Through Preservation board members and tour chairmen. We paused at the rear of the school to gaze through Johnson's eyes at Aster Avenue, Firestone Park's business district. We saw a Dairy Mart, but to Johnson it was the Circle Theater, where she saw movies for fourteen cents until 1951 or 1952. During her growing-up years, the district still supported two more markets, a Lucky Shoes store, an Acme, a five-and-ten-cent store, and several restaurants. Her favorite was Tenpennies, where she could buy a hamburger, fries, and a shake for forty-five cents.

JANUARY 16, 2000

On Blue Pond

Did you know that Blue Pond is bottomless and connects underground with White Pond? That was the urban legend when Lori Michalec was a pupil at Goodyear Middle School in Akron. She was Lori Fish then—the late 1970s—and lived in the Goodyear Heights neighborhood surrounding the pond. We met Michalec, now a secretary at the school, when we went looking for signs of the amusement park that once thrived on Blue Pond's shores.

For those who've never heard of Blue Pond, it's across Johns Avenue from the school and occupies the middle of a triangle formed by Goodyear Boulevard, East Market Street, and the old Norfolk & Western railroad tracks. It's also about six miles—as the crow flies—east of White Pond, which lies just west of the Akron boundary line in Copley Township, so the underground-connection tale seems far-fetched. But it was a dynamite conversation starter.

We stopped at the office to get permission to view the pond from the school's hilltop property. We got more than we bargained for. Michalec asked if we'd ever heard about the train that sank to the bottom of the pond when its trestle collapsed. That was the tale her grandmother, Anna Fish of Lakemore, used to tell. "She said the trestle kept sinking over the years, and eventually the train fell in," Michalec said.

Education assistant Terri Cheatham Easterwood told us she attended the school, too, from 1969 to 1971. She recalled the pond, which was off-limits to pupils, as the place where "the boys met after school to smoke." Chuck, who attended the school in the early 1960s, when it was still Goodyear Junior High, recalled that boys would meet there to settle disputes with fisticuffs. They still do, Michalec said. "They meet under the bridge," she said, referring to the one that carries Goodyear Boulevard into the valley in which the pond and railroad tracks lie.

Neither woman had heard about the amusement park, and Chuck and I had to admit we knew little ourselves. We all knew the park predated the school, which was built as East High School in 1918 and became a junior high when the new East High opened in 1955. The best information we found was a July 11, 1990 letter to the editor written by retired *Beacon Journal* sports writer Phillip J. Dietrich. After reading an article stating the park's closing date was unknown, Dietrich went to the library, found some details in the September 15, 1898, edition of the *Summit County Beacon* and shared some of the text: "Blue Pond Park, the once locally famous pleasure resort, is slowly falling into decay. . . . The boathouse would not be recognized as such and the pier, which extends into the lake a short distance, has sunk until it is almost totally submerged." The story said the park was built around 1892 at a cost of $26,000, and that by 1898 the stockholders were broke.

Apparently the park was already a dim memory by 1925, when *A Centennial History of Akron* was published by the Summit County Historical Society. The book contains one passing reference: ". . . to the east we find Blue Pond, a body of water of considerable size whose northern bank was a favorite spot

Goodyear Middle School can be seen across Blue Pond.

for recreation and picnics many years ago; while during the winter months its ice was much enjoyed by skating parties."

Our impromptu history class came to order when Judy Canova, principal of the 780-pupil school, came into the office. Learning of our mission, she graciously allowed us to peek at the pond from the third-floor classroom where Yolanda Green teaches eighth-grade algebra. The view was good from that elevation, but we decided a better one awaited across the pond on a street appropriately named Pondview. From there, the pond looked much as it might have before civilization arrived—if water and foliage were all you looked at. The school dominated the horizon across the water, but the Goodyear tower was visible through the trees. We walked to the bridge beneath which the boys meet to fight and found another spectacular view, looking south across the water at the sprawl of the Goodyear complex, East High, and the Airdock.

We left without learning anything new about Blue Pond and asking another question: How did it get its name? For that matter, how were White Pond, Black Pond, and Yellow Pond named? Sounds like fodder for another story.

JANUARY 7, 1990

Swan Lake

There was never any question about who ruled the lake. Big and bossy, the swan swam over as soon as we appeared on the western shore, and all the other waterfowl made room. We walked the western shore of Summit Lake in southwest Akron because it afforded greater pedestrian access and because neither of us had ever looked at the lake from that perspective. It also was our first close encounter with a swan.

"He's nasty," warned Pete Jones of Brady Avenue, one of ten short streets between Manchester Road and Summit Lake Boulevard west of the ninety-three-acre lake.

The birds approach all comers in search of handouts, said Jones, who was walking Heidi, his fourteen-year-old German shepherd, when we arrived. But they scatter when the bullying swan comes near—all but a large white goose who is believed to nest with the swan somewhere in the tall winter-brown swamp grass and cattails that line the shore. The beggars included scores of gulls, mallards, Canada geese, and a species we had never seen before—chicken-sized, web-footed black birds with pointy white beaks. A reference book later revealed them to be American coots.

Our feathery entourage floated south at a safe distance from the swan, which hugged the bank as we walked in the same direction. When we stopped, the birds did, too. It happened several times until the bully brazenly left the water for a closer look at us. It was a graceless exit, a labored waddle, and I was tempted to look away as one might to spare the feelings of an embarrassed person. Then I laughed, reminding myself this was, after all, a dumb bird. When he was satisfied we had no food, the swan struggled back to the water, which he entered with a graceful glide through a corridor cleared by the other birds.

We continued moving south in search of an artist's vantage point, putting the birds out of mind until we heard a loud splashing behind us. Turning, we witnessed a demonstration of power unlike anything either of us had ever experienced. It was the swan taking to the air in a way reminiscent of an old propeller-driven airliner. His feet pumped the water, and his wings flapped furiously for several yards as he built up speed. Then he stretched his neck straight forward and began to rise, slowly at first, his feet splashing the water's surface, then faster and higher, his wings making a humming sound and his feet tucked close to his body.

The swan's destination was clear in a moment. Two people stood on the southeastern shore, and the swan no doubt sensed a handout. He flew straight as an arrow across the lake and scattered the birds gathered there. Soon, the coots, gulls, mallards, and geese abandoned us, too, leaving us to walk unnoticed except by a cat who seemed to be stalking something in the brush along the shore.

I left the artist drawing near a downed tree that sprawled close to the water's edge and ventured on alone, careful to avoid bird and dog droppings that littered the landscape. They seemed less intrusive to the environment than what was left by humans—pop and beer containers, an old tricycle, and sheets of plastic. People have been dumping stuff in Summit Lake since they arrived at its shores. Industrial pollution robbed the water of its oxygen and rendered it virtually useless for years before many nearby factories closed. Major fish kills were frequently reported during the 1930s, 1940s, and 1950s. Stolen vehicles, including a $30,000 backhoe taken in 1981 from Margaret Park School on the northwest shore, have been abandoned in the water.

Houses line the west side of Summit Lake Boulevard, which is a misnomer for the short, narrow street that runs along the western side of Summit Lake from Trail Street on the north to Harvey Avenue on the south. Most of the homes appear to be well maintained, and some appear to have been built within the last twenty years. A couple near the north end of the street are quite elaborate. A road with an equally curious name was First Street Southwest, which describes what is little more than a rutted path at the south end of the lake. It runs in a southerly direction from Harvey through some brush to Kenmore Boulevard. There are few signs of the summer playground that flourished at Summit Lake in previous decades. Across from a boat launch ramp at Thelma Avenue and the boulevard is an asphalt-shingled building that once housed a canoe livery, according to Pete Jones. A sign at the ramp warns:

> No Wake
> No Swimming
> No Waterskiing

Just north of that is the remnant of a private wooden dock, with a section nearest the shore partly submerged, leaving two other sections standing isolated in the water.

A hotel once stood at the corner of Brady and the boulevard, Jones said. Its patrons arrived by interurban cars that ran on one of two lines that served the lake. The other line ran to the east shore, where Lakeside Park of the early 1900s evolved into Summit Beach Park, a popular amusement center that lasted until 1959.

The city of Akron began buying and improving property on both shores and, today, operates a community center, two ball fields, and a soccer field at the north end of the lake. Akron also owns a canoe livery on the east shore near Ira Avenue and Lakeshore Boulevard. The water quality has improved as industry in the area has declined, and fishing is said to be good these days. We saw two fishermen in separate boats the day we were there. The city's 1978 master plan calls for a marina to be built some day, at the north end of Summit Lake. That property is owned by the State of Ohio, which also owns the lake—on paper, that is.

Recalling our white-feathered friend, we know who the real owner is.

APRIL 12, 1998

Easter Is Their Big Day

A niche in a wall at St. Mary's Catholic Church in Akron bears an inscription proclaiming beliefs churches celebrate throughout the world today as most Christians observe Easter. It is a New Testament quotation taken from the tenth chapter of Paul's letter to the Romans: "For if thou confess with thy mouth the Lord Jesus and believe in thy heart that God hath raised him from the dead, thou shalt be saved, for with the heart we believe unto justice but with the mouth confession is made unto salvation."

We found the inscription on a walk that seemed to have an Easter theme. We decided to explore a section of Akron where churches dominate the skyline. We started at Thornton and South Main streets, where St. Mary's is located, because of that church's impressive tower and because we could think of three other churches that were visible from there. We were conservative in our estimate. We counted seven from a small hill in a park between St. Mary's and Riedinger Middle School at 77 West Thornton. We couldn't identify all of them from where we were standing, so we went looking for their names and addresses, walking to the ones nearby and driving in search of the others. Along the way, we found three more.

Congregations have been celebrating Easter at St. Mary's since 1887—since 1915 in the present church, said Rev. John J. Hilkert, pastor for thirty-two years. I had been at the church a few times before, but it wasn't until Chuck and I walked its grounds that I spotted the niche and its inscription.

Across Main Street at the Church of the Good Shepherd (United Methodist) worship has been conducted since 1882. Back then, the church was called Main Street Methodist Episcopal. Church historian Stewart Steiner told us the original building was replaced by the present church in 1924. The new name dates to 1978, when members of Calvary United Brethren Church on Coburn Street and Main Street Methodist formed a new church. Chuck and I noticed the large sign in front of Good Shepherd is blank on one side, which makes sense when you consider that this section of Main is a one-way street and doesn't have any traffic heading north.

The other nearby churches were the Original Church of God, a block south at 807 Coburn; the River of Life Church, a block east at 90 West Thornton; and the Second Baptist Church, a block north at 690 South Main.

The distant churches were more of a challenge, but in finding them we saw their environments in a new light. We went looking for churches and discovered neighborhoods we'd driven through many times but had never really seen. This was especially true along the streets off Thornton between Main and the innerbelt, where houses were a blend of old and new. In the middle of all this, we found the Yale A.O.H. Church of God. It wasn't much bigger than the homes that surrounded it, and we would never have spotted it had we not driven down Yale.

We drove to the east end of Thornton at Spicer Street and found no churches. But to the south we could better see the two remaining churches we had spotted from St. Mary's: Sacred Heart of Jesus at 734 Grant Street and St. Paul Fire Baptized Holiness at 745 Wolf Ledges Parkway. We also spotted two others: New Beginnings Family Church on South Street near

Churches dominate the south Akron skyline.

Washington Street and Concordia Lutheran Church at Sumner and Voris Streets. Concordia and its parking lot occupy one short block of Sumner between Voris and the pedestrian walkway over Interstates 76 and 77. The other side of the street is filled with six nicely maintained homes that appear to date to the post-World War I population boom in Akron.

On our way back to Main Street, we spotted the Goodyear blimp cutting its way through the gray clouds, and Chuck screeched his car to a halt. We waited until it drifted over St. Paul Fire Baptized Holiness and Sacred Heart of Jesus churches so he could capture what we decided would be a perfect postscript to our story.

OCTOBER 4, 1987

Strolling along Triplett Hill

Even if you have seen them scores of times before, the Rubber Bowl, Derby Downs, Akron-Fulton Municipal Airport, and the Airdock are breathtaking from the top of Triplett Hill. After walking east along Triplett Boulevard through the rather unremarkable looking residential and commercial neighborhood between Arlington Street and Kelly Avenue, one welcomes the first view of the huge green sprawl that encompasses these four Akron landmarks.

That isn't a putdown of the Thomastown neighborhood, named for a hamlet that was part of an annexation to Akron nearly sixty years ago. It is home to several thousand people and the place where several thousand more earn their daily bread. Among the details that might escape notice if the trip were made by car are the white Thunderbird parked on the devil strip next to the sign that bans parking on the devil strip, the bird's nest in the Fruehauf sign, and the chatter of air-driven equipment used in the company's truck terminal. The smell of hot tar fills the air as you approach the Blossom Hill Apartments, which are all but hidden by tall shrubs. The source is discovered at the Baltimore Avenue entrance to the apartment parking lot, where workmen are making repairs.

The scene to the east suddenly changes as you approach the Thomastown Party Center at 1280 Triplett. You're high enough to be looking down on the rooftop of the Coca-Cola plant in the valley below. And beyond it are the four landmarks. But you don't see them all at once when you're walking. First you see the giant letters that spell "A-K-R-O-N." Then, in small sections, the airport, the Rubber Bowl, Derby Downs, and, finally, when you're just east of 1300 Triplett, the Airdock. Somehow it seems fitting to view the scene from in front of the building at 1300. The raised letters over its front door were removed years ago, but if you look carefully you can make out the words "Daniel Guggenheim Airship Institute."

Art deco in style and the scene of some of lighter-than-air's most exciting brainstorming in the 1920s and 1930s, the building was sold by Goodyear and became headquarters for Junior Achievement. Pat Masturzo and Donald Johns, owners of the party center, bought it in 1980 and now use it for office and storage space eleven months out of the year. People are more likely to recognize the place as the Haunted Laboratory, which it becomes every October. Masturzo and Johns employ 175 high school students and ten adult supervisors there and at the party center, which has been the Haunted Schoolhouse each October since 1975.

The party center was built as Thomastown School in 1921, when the hamlet was part of Springfield Township. The Akron Public Schools took it over in 1930 after the annexation of land between Massillon and Arlington roads in Springfield and Coventry townships. During World War II, as a branch of Hower Vocational High, the school was headquarters for training aircraft mechanics. The school system remodeled it in 1949 and repaired it in 1956 after vandals set it afire. It was put on the auction block after Clinton D. Barrett School opened in 1972.

High on Triplett Hill on dark October nights, the moon hangs bright over the alley. It's a proper place for Halloween ghosts and goblins to gather. And for those who love to study the stars, it's the perfect spot to point a telescope toward the heavens.

Akron landmarks line Triplett Boulevard.

Walking Lovers Lane

A walk down Lovers Lane in Akron is a study in urban change. It is a short street, just a mile between Wilbur Avenue on the west and Arlington Street on the east, and named, no doubt, for an activity practiced by the young and romantic when Lovers Lane was a dirt track on the southern edge of town. Wilbur and eight other streets intersect with it before Lovers Lane reaches the bridge over Interstate 77, which creates, perhaps, the greatest change in the landscape. Twelve more streets empty into Lovers Lane before it terminates at Arlington.

It is on this collection of tree-lined streets that people whose surnames originated in such places as Russia, Poland, and Yugoslavia settled in homes within walking distance of Goodyear and Firestone, where husbands worked, and where wives bought groceries, dry goods, hardware, and other household needs. Some of these families stayed. Many others moved on, to be replaced by younger families starting out on life's adventure. Many of the shops are gone, but the ones that remain help maintain the residential character of the neighborhood.

Lovers Lane is a street of trees, large oaks, many of which arch over the street and some of which have been sculpted into unnatural shapes to accommodate utility lines. A utility pole at Hammel Street is decorated with the rusting heads of hundreds of nails, no doubt from fliers heralding everything from political candidates to garage sales. Skating would be tough along many of the raised and cracked sidewalks on Lovers Lane. In contrast, wheelchair access was added when new walks were poured at some intersections.

Lovers Lane is a street of churches. A store once occupied the northwest corner of Lovers Lane and Inman Street. Today it is the home of the Bible Baptist Evangelical Center. A sign at Lovers Lane Christian Church reminds us that "Fools and dead men don't change their minds. Fools won't. Dead men can't."

If Lovers Lane has a mercantile district, it is the short stretch between Ada and Inman Streets, where Milandy's Cafe and the Belmont Grill comfortably coexist and Killian's Super Market and John's Canvas Products are landmarks. Weather permitting, Dan Bogunovich has his morning coffee on the sidewalk in front of the awning shop. It gives him a chance to catch up on news of the neighborhood with passersby. Bogunovich has been in business there six years. His father-in-law, John Treitinger, has owned the building at 773 Lovers Lane for more than forty years.

"It's still a nice neighborhood," Bogunovich said, "but it changed a lot after I-77 came through. In the old days, everybody had beautiful gardens."

The market across the street has been owned by Bruce and Mary Ann Killian since 1986, although they have run it since 1974 and he has worked there since 1969, his senior year at Hoban High.

"I bought the building from the butcher, Alex Hardy, when he retired," Killian said. "He was here more than forty years."

Forty-four years, to be exact, said Hardy, who, with Killian, helped construct a history of the market. A butcher named Joe Amstadt owned the building and leased grocery space to Acme when Hardy went to work there in 1942. Hardy bought the building when Amstadt moved to California in 1944. He and his wife, Mary, operated the meat department and continued the lease arrangement with Acme until 1969. In the early years, the Hardys walked to work from their home around the corner on Bertha Avenue. After 1959, they commuted from Springfield Township, where they still live. Dave Bryant (then Akron City Council president), who is married to the Hardys' daughter, Janet, was a longtime employee. Kroger's had a store nearby for a few years, Hardy recalled. Within easy walking distance were a bakery, two barbershops, shoe and TV repair shops, a dry cleaner, and drug and hardware stores.

"Lovers Lane was just a dirt track when the first barbershop opened," said Killian, who is too young to know that firsthand but has heard the story for as long as he can remember. "People had to walk to Arlington Street to pick up their mail, and it was all woods back (south) to Wilbeth."

the original building in 1903, when the school was part of the Coventry system.

First stop along the boulevard was the Coffee Shop, where everybody in Kenmore stops for breakfast or lunch. Ken Zehenni, son of owners Zuker and Yvonne Zehenni, was behind the counter and unfazed by our group. We declined his offer of a cool drink but stopped long enough to meet seventy-four-year-old Ellen Benn, a regular customer who credits Kenmore's children with keeping her young. She is also, we learned, the mother of artist Dave Benn, a friend who teaches at Innes Middle School. Back on the street, we hurried past a bookstore (to my regret) to peer in the windows of a tattoo parlor, which was called Z Tattoo.

We became two groups as some youngsters hung back to watch Chuck sketch while the rest pressed ahead. James Haag and Justin Estep put their sketchbooks to use. Emily Rodriguez and Michelle Hummel confided that they want to be reporters.

The artists caught up with the wordsmiths at the candy store. It really is McDowell's Pharmacy, but penny candy is the feature that attracted our guides. We put together enough money to finance ten cents worth of candy for each member of our party. In the most orderly fashion, the ten-year-olds lined up, selected their treats, said thank you, and waited out on the sidewalk for the group to reassemble. While she was waiting on her customers, Liz McDowell gave a mini-history of the family business, which was started in 1920 by her grandfather, Vance McDowell. Her father, John McDowell, the pharmacist, was busy in the rear of the tiny store, so we didn't bother him.

The children were eager to show us Miller's Hobby Shop, which is next door to the Ohio College of Massotherapy. Reymann pointed out that the building housing the massage training center was once a movie theater. Josh McCombs said he's a regular at the hobby shop. Next to Miller's is another favorite haunt, Kenmore Komics. The adults in the party overruled a motion to go inside.

There is a moment in every one of these adventures when Chuck or I will take a backward glance or round a corner and make a discovery that sets the walk apart from all others. The pleasure was mine in Kenmore, when I discovered Lee and Jasper McCutchan's garden, a small terraced lot between the comic-book store and the building housing McCutchan's Heating and Air Conditioning. There's a fancy wrought-iron gate across the front and another along the back on Florida Avenue. The lot has been planted with grass, shrubs, and flowers worthy of any house and garden tour. A round table and some chairs on the brick patio complete the tableau.

"This used to be a trash dump," said Mrs. McCutchan, who came outside when she saw us stop. "The girls from Ohio College (of Massotherapy) come here for lunch." Then she insisted that all thirty of us come inside to see her office, which was filled with enough homey touches to make one forget that it once was a storefront.

Kathi Rose and Alisha Findley became our guides when we rounded the corner onto Florida. They were eager to point out their homes, which could be seen from McCutchan's garden. The backs of Kenmore Boulevard buildings, while not as attractive as their fronts, are interesting. McCutchan's is artistically treated both in color and design. The day was warm, so we were able to peek through an open door at the Crawford Bindery at Fourteenth and Florida; Brian Jeffries pointed out where his mother, Betty Jeffries, works. A cat silently watched our parade from a front porch, while a man cutting his lawn yelled at some of the children who had left the sidewalk to walk along his stone wall.

We saw churches—the Chapel of Hope, at 706 Florida; Goss Memorial, 100 feet away at Eleventh and Florida, where Jeremy Powell is a member; and United Wesleyan, at Ninth and Florida. The former Boulevard Methodist, at Seventh and Kenmore, is now Bruce Ferrini's and Denis Conley's 754 Gallery.

Our last stop, next door to the school, was Robert Schutte's Ace Lock Company. There we visited with Bill Arnold, whom Reymann described as Kenmore's historian. Arnold was born on Eleventh Street across from Goss Memorial Church and lives on the boulevard, next door to the key shop. His father, the late Claude Arnold, started the Kenmore Board of Trade.

The dismissal bell at the school was about to ring so we were excused for the day. No grades were given out, but if we had our way, the class would get straight A's.

DECEMBER 10, 2000

Nob Hill

A line from an old song—"... the last rose of summer left blooming all alone ..."—came to mind as we arrived at Bastogne and Dickemery drives in northwest Akron. Spotting a pale yellow rose still blooming on a bush that grew around a pole topped by the two street signs, I thought, this bud's for you, Mike Bucalo. We were there because Bucalo, a *Beacon Journal* reader, had called to ask a question: How did Dickemery, Bastogne, and the neighborhood's third street, Nob Hill Drive, come by their names? Bucalo said he had recently bought a house in the neighborhood off Upper Merriman Drive and had been told Bastogne was named for the Belgian city that was besieged in the World War II Battle of the Bulge. He wondered if Dickemery might have been named in honor of a casualty of that war.

Close, but not quite the case, we learned, but the story that unfolded after our visit is just as interesting. The neighborhood is sandwiched between two sets of railroad tracks, the Wheeling & Lake Erie on the west and the Cuyahoga Valley on the east. The valley is just east of the second set of tracks, and the only way into and out of the neighborhood is on Bastogne, which begins at a bend in Upper Merriman, just west of the Wheeling & Lake Erie tracks.

A huge rock on the lawn of a hilltop home at the gateway to the neighborhood bears a weathered metal nameplate that spells out "n-o-b h-i-l-l" in large lower-case letters. The rock looks as if it has been there forever and the sign only slightly less time. The terrain on which the home was built appears to have answered part of Bucalo's question.

Lady Liberty, a people-sized replica of the statue that greets ships arriving at New York harbor, graces the front lawn at a residence on Bastogne, across

Nob Hill Drive is seen from two perspectives.

the street from the rosebush-covered street sign. This Liberty's torch electrically lights the driveway at night.

The most remarkable thing about the neighborhood is its location. It looks upscale suburban. Make that exurban, with backyards that disappear in the valley's rolling hills. But it's in the heart of the city, just a short drive or slightly long walk away from downtown Akron. Dickemery is the least interesting of the streets. It's a very lovely street, but because it's sandwiched between Nob Hill and Bastogne, its backyards back on to other backyards instead of forest. There's actually a fourth street, Ravine View Drive, which is separated from the others. It parallels the Wheeling & Lake Erie tracks, and looks like a recent addition to the enclave. We had driven past it without noticing it and really saw it only when we were on foot.

A man cutting fallen trees along the tracks, seventy-seven-year-old Clyde Dye, said he lives just outside the neighborhood, at Upper Merriman and Bastogne, and didn't know the origin of the street names. It took only two phone calls after our walk to solve the puzzle. I called longtime Akron Symphony volunteer Gladys Snell, who, I discovered, lives in the neighborhood. She referred me to veteran travel agent C. P. Chima, who, I was surprised to discover, was one of the neighborhood's developers. Part of what caller Bucalo had heard was confirmed by Chima: Nob Hill, as the development was called, was started by Chima and three other World War II veterans to meet the postwar housing needs. The other partners were William R. McClenathen, who, like Chima, flew bombers for the Air Force during the war; Byron Fry, who had been a Navy pilot; and Richard Emery, who had been a sergeant in the Army.

A surveyor hired by the partners likened the area at the entrance of the neighborhood to San Francisco's Nob Hill, thus the name, Chima said. McClenathen flew missions over Bastogne, so he named that street.

What about Dickemery?

"Since Bill, Byron, and I were all pilots, Dick decided he wanted to learn to fly, too," Chima said. Emery had logged about twenty hours in the air when he crashed the plane he was flying near Cambridge just as Nob Hill was getting started, so the street was named in his memory, Chima said.

Real estate wasn't the partners' only postwar venture. Before Nob Hill, they were among the founders of the G. I. Cab Company, which today is operated by McClenathen's son, Derek.

As reservists, McClenathen, Fry, and Chima were called back into service during the Korean War, and the sixty-five-acre Nob Hill development was completed by others. One thing Chima didn't mention but which I discovered in the *Beacon Journal* archives: on one of his forty-four flying missions over Europe, this last surviving member of the development team was awarded the Silver Star for his rescue of a colleague's crippled B-17.

CHAPTER FIVE

Akron's University, a Work in Progress

Of all the places Chuck and I explored since our series began in 1987, the University of Akron was the most complex in its ever-changing nature. We saw the university stretch skyward with the construction of modern buildings that harmonize with some of the community's oldest structures, and expand west to Main Street with the adaptive reuse of the landmark Polsky Building. And we realized, even as we recorded our most recent visit in 1999, that what we were seeing was just the latest installment in a continuing story of development.

AUGUST 6, 1989

Once around the Campus

For all its newness, the University of Akron's Buchtel Mall (now called Buchtel Common) evokes as many memories as it does reactions to itself. Quite by accident, we picked freshman orientation day for our visit to the pedestrian walkway that stretches between Sumner Street from the foot of the new Polymer Science Building east to the point where Brown and South

Union streets meet. As a result, the mall was crowded with incoming students and many of their parents.

We approached from Grant Street, walking along a block of Buchtel Avenue still open to motor vehicles, but which will eventually become part of the mall. Standing on the sidewalk in front of Whitby Hall at 200 East Buchtel, we felt the first of a flood of memories surface as we took our first close up look at the Polymer Science Building across the street. It so dominates the point of the flatiron block bordered by East Center, Buchtel, and Grant Streets that we stood there for several minutes before the artist realized that this was where he had spent more than three years teaching art before the graphic design department was moved to the former Dave Towell Cadillac building on East Exchange Street.

From where we stood, we discovered a new view of Akron's skyline—a view combining one of Akron's newest buildings with one of its older ones, St. Bernard's Catholic Church. But if the view was good, it got better as we mounted the steps to the third floor of the Auburn Science and Engineering Center to reach the skywalk that links Auburn to the polymer building. The skywalk hadn't opened except for use by the construction crews, but we ventured out to the middle for our first real look at the mall. The view was dramatic and one few had yet seen, but it excluded the polymer building, so we decided to walk across the tree-lined upper campus—the walkway between Carroll and Buchtel—to see the mall from the east end before actually walking down it. The shade and a slight breeze eased the effects of the humidity and eighty-five-degree heat and spread the fragrances of flowers growing in beds in front of a bookstore branch housed in the former ROTC building. That brought back another memory for Chuck, a Kent State graduate. He spent his freshman year at the University of Akron, which had a mandatory ROTC membership. Perhaps it was the paisley more than a few students were wearing on this day that sent us on a nostalgia trip of how we spent October 15, 1969, the so-called day of moratorium against the Vietnam War. But fresh yellow and black paint on a giant rock brought us back to 1989. *Batman* was about to open in Akron movie theaters and already the caped crusader's logo was a part of the campus landscape.

At the mall's east end, Chuck found his view and shared another memory—of driving past the fire station, which stood for nearly fifty years at Brown and Buchtel, the morning after racial disturbances brought National Guard troops to Akron in July 1968. A curfew had cleared the streets, and his car was the only one on the road. An armed sentry sitting in the open doorway of the fire station was the only other person he saw as he drove to work.

While the artist began his work, I ventured onto the new brick walk to do mine, passing more parents of freshmen and a few faculty members I recognized from earlier visits to the campus. An elderly woman dressed in more than one layer of clothing and wearing a baseball batting helmet asked for directions to Union Street. I resisted the urge to inquire about her outfit and simply pointed the way. Another pedestrian who caught my eye was a young man, whose roots could probably be traced to the Indian subcontinent, shading himself with an umbrella.

A statue of John R. Buchtel, whose money established Buchtel College, and a new fountain stand at the middle of the mall—the statue on the south side, with its back to Buchtel Hall, and the fountain on the north, where College Street ends. Chuck Rader, a workman for the Cavanaugh Building Corporation, was sweeping sand into the cracks between the paving bricks and chuckling about the soap suds that someone had dumped into the fountain. "We made a real campus out of this, didn't we?" Rader said, echoing thoughts we had had at the start of the walk. Cavanaugh is to complete its work by the end of the year. The $500,000 project was first proposed by university officials more than twenty years ago but failed to win approval because city officials were concerned about the traffic problems it might create.

The University of Akron's Buchtel Common was new when we visited in 1989.

APRIL 7, 1991

Exploring the Towers

Viewed up close from the sidewalk, the University of Akron's Polymer Science Building looks like a big glass box. That perspective offers no hint of the not-so-identical twin towers' real shape or what awaits inside. The center, which was dedicated just six days ago, has been high on our list of neighborhoods to explore. It is the city's newest and, at a price tag of $17 million, among the most expensive. It also will be one of the most exclusive neighborhoods around. Because government research will be conducted on its upper levels, floors four through twelve will be closed to the public. So we decided we would, while we could, take you for a vertical stroll around the university's center for polymer research.

It was library quiet in the lobby, which connects the twelve-story east tower with its nine-story twin to the west. The color scheme is simple—gray walls and carpeting and yellow handrails on stairways that rise three flights up the east tower and five flights up the west. Standing on the first landing of the east staircase, looking up, Chuck was reminded of the stark visions of angles and curves at the Kennedy Space Center.

It was impossible to walk the stairs from top to bottom because of scaffolding and other work still in progress. But we were otherwise free to explore the then-unoccupied regions under the guidance of Roger Ryan, UA vice president for administrative services, and university police officer Marilyn Firestone. We started at the top. Ryan took us by freight elevator to the twelfth floor and what he called the "captured space" between the towers. Imagine the towers as individual buildings thirty feet apart and connected at each floor from the first through the ninth. By using a sloped roof, architect Richard Fleischman was able to extend the east tower's tenth, eleventh, and twelfth floors to the west even though the west tower stops after nine floors. The result was usable space not originally planned for. The twelfth-floor conference room overlooks an eleventh-floor study area that extends farther out

Downtown Akron as we saw it from the Polymer Science Building.

because of the sloped roof. And the extended tenth-floor space is larger than the space on the eleventh floor.

From the twelfth-floor conference room, the university's link to downtown Akron was more pronounced than we had seen before. The eye is drawn from the new traffic circle at the base of the building westward along University Street (formerly Center Street), over the bridge that spans the tracks to Broadway, High, and Main Streets and beyond. From the stillness of this interior vantage point, we looked out on a city alive with motion—people on foot, cars, buses, a southbound train from Quaker Square, and even a fire engine. Looking north, one can see the Coliseum (the Richfield sports center that has since been razed) and virtually everything in between. E. J. Thomas Performing Arts Hall sprawls like a giant fan below. Its multilevel plaza on the south end, so easy to overlook from the ground, looks inviting from twelve stories up.

Looking down from the south side of the conference room, one sees an artistic network of silver-colored ductwork atop the roof of the chemistry building and the growing skeleton of the biology research building under construction adjacent to the Auburn Science Center. The view beyond encompasses the southern half of the campus, including dormitories, a motel-turned-dormitory, and an auto dealership-turned-art department, and the city toward the southern horizon. A laboratory on the top floor of the east tower affords a spectacular view of Buchtel Common's serpentine path eastward from the circle in front of the building.

Scaffolding blocked the stairways between floors twelve and six, so we took the elevator to the fifth floor, where the towers are again connected. Here we found the building's most spectacular view, from the top of the west tower's atrium down to the lobby. On the third floor of the east tower we walked through the administrative office and then took another set of stairs down to the second floor, where we visited a classroom large enough to seat forty. Before Ryan left us to our own devices, he showed us the 213-seat Goodyear Tire & Rubber Company Auditorium at the east end of the east tower. It is terraced and has entrances from two floors. We saw it from a balcony high above the stage.

We encountered few people during more than two hours of exploring the building, and yet we left with the feeling that it would remain just as quiet when it is fully occupied by two hundred students and scientists.

DECEMBER 18, 1999

Buchtel Hall Builds on Past

It was a happy coincidence that we visited the University of Akron campus on the same day (November 30, 1999) ground was broken for the first stage of a six-year, $200 million campus makeover. We didn't see the ceremony, which took place just north of E. J. Thomas Performing Arts Hall, or even know about it until we read the *Beacon Journal* the next morning. But the event dovetailed nicely with the yesterday-today-and-tomorrow storytelling focus of our walks around town.

We were drawn to the campus by the yesterday aspect of that equation— the fact that tomorrow marks the one-hundredth anniversary of the fire that destroyed the original Buchtel Hall, the five-story building in which Buchtel College thrived for its first twenty-seven years. The present Buchtel Hall, built on the same hilltop to replace the original, was dedicated in 1901 and is the oldest attraction UA has to offer, so we set out to find the best angle from which to view it. The traffic circle at the south end of College Street, just below the Buchtel Common, came to mind, but we decided to first look at Buchtel Hall from a distance. So we began hoofing it east up Mill Street, leaving footprints in the season's first layer of snow. We found the best angle at the crest of the hill on the Mill Street bridge. Dark clouds moving in from the north promised to deliver the additional flurries that were forecast, but the sun poked through the lighter-shaded cloudbank that hung above the southern horizon, bathing the campus in a light that begged to be captured on film or canvas.

Buchtel Hall didn't dominate the skyline, but it held its own against the glass-walled Goodyear Polymer Center, E. J. Thomas Hall, and other familiar

UA landmarks. From where we stood, E. J. Thomas poked its head above the salmon-and-beige Olson Research Center, which is named for UA benefactors Sidney and Miriam Olson. The 72,340-square-foot former Olson Electronics warehouse has been home to the university's polymer engineering department since 1983. The groundbreaking we missed was for a four-story, $6 million Polymer Engineering Academic Center that will be connected to the Olson buildings by a walkway. The artist's perspective also showed the campus in the context of the city that has grown up around it since 1870, when the Ohio Universalist Church founded its coed liberal arts college on Middlebury Road (later Buchtel Avenue and now Buchtel Common).

Below us on the railroad tracks, a parked train began to move slowly to the south. It was so long we couldn't see its front or back or even hear its engine. From around the bend came a northbound train, moving faster than the other. It was also shorter and was soon upon us, then beyond us, then out of sight. At the east end of the bridge, where Mill intersects Lincoln Street, we looked over the guardrail and saw what appeared to be a squatter's shelter—a tent-sized cardboard box that was open on one side and from which emerged a quilt and other personal belongings. No occupant was in sight.

Just past Lincoln, before College Street and parallel to them both, we came upon a short unmarked alley that dead ends at the thrift shop at the rear of the Wonder Bread-Hostess building on Forge Street. What caught our eye was an apparently occupied home, the only residence in an otherwise commercial area. We walked down the alley for a closer look at the house, which was gray with green trim and black shutters and had snow-covered mums still blooming in a narrow flowerbed below the front porch. The address—103—was displayed on the front porch, leading us to wonder if the alley had a name. We asked a clerk at the bread company thrift store, but she didn't know. We checked our city maps, including one from 1870, but found no name. We hit pay dirt when we checked the 1917 Akron directory in the *Beacon Journal* reference department. The alley is—or at least was—called Price Place.

Buchtel Hall came into view again as we rounded the corner at College

Three illustrations show (inset) the Polymer Science Building and Buchtel Hall on the University of Akron campus.

Street and headed south. The Stars and Stripes and the Ohio and UA flags waved in the breeze from a single staff out front, and we noted, as we reached the Buchtel Common, that the bigger-than-life statue of UA founder John R. Buchtel was plastered with wet snow. The most impressive sight of the day was the cityscape reflected against the east wall of the Polymer Building. The sky to the west was gray, but the glass wall reflected the blue sky to the east and some fast-moving billows of white clouds.

Looking at Buchtel Hall, we were reminded of descriptions we had read of the original five-story building. Akron historian Samuel Lane devoted nineteen pages to Buchtel College in *Fifty Years and Over of Akron and Summit County,* which was published in 1892, seven years before the fire. Lane began by saying, "This institution is the crowning educational glory of Akron, and, indeed, of Summit County, since the ruthless spoilation (*sic*) of the venerated old Western Reserve College at Hudson, and requires more than a passing mention in this work." (Lane was obviously still fuming over the decision to move Western Reserve College—now Case Western Reserve University—to Cleveland.)

UA historian George Knepper, in his 1990 book *Summit's Glory: Sketches of Buchtel College and the University of Akron,* wrote of the original Buchtel Hall, "It loomed over the city and dominated it.... Throughout its twenty-seven years it remained the most impressive structure that most of its occupants had ever seen."

The five-story building was 240 feet long, 54 feet wide, and had twin towers through which entrances led into east and west wings. Male students lived in the east wing, female students in the west. The building also had a chapel that could seat several hundred, lecture halls, a library, a gymnasium, a dining room, and a kitchen.

Among the fascinating tidbits in Knepper's book is the fact that Buchtel College was built on the site of the Spicer Hill Cemetery, which was replaced by the Akron Rural—now Glendale—Cemetery. Knepper said "at least sixty-four bodies were transferred to Akron Rural before ground was broken for the College building on March 15, 1871."

New York Tribune editor Horace Greeley was the featured speaker when the cornerstone of the original Buchtel Hall was laid on July 4, 1871, and the lobby of the present Buchtel Hall is named for him.

On December 20, 1899, shortly before 5 P.M. on the day before the fall term ended, a man ran into the west wing, interrupting a faculty meeting, and shouting that the building was on fire, Knepper wrote. Akron's entire fire department responded to the alarm, but the fire spread quickly and within three hours only the building's shell remained.

The community responded to the college's needs and began collecting money immediately to rebuild. Crouse Gymnasium, called "the finest gym west of the Alleghenies" when it was dedicated in 1888, became the center of learning, with some classes also being held in the president's residence and nearby businesses.

Buchtel College kept growing in the new century. It became the Municipal University of Akron in 1913 and has been a state university since 1967. Growth in the twenty-first century will include a $41 million student center, scheduled to open before the end of 2001, five additional buildings, an open-space expansion to sixty acres, and the proposed closing of Carroll and Union Streets on campus.

CHAPTER SIX

Strolling through Parks, Big and Small

It seems a bit silly to consider communing with nature as work, but that was part of our job description when Chuck and I gathered impressions for these pieces. In fact, our walks in the park best exemplify a recurring question we asked each other throughout our travels: Can you believe they're paying us to do this? Yes, we enjoyed the experiences enormously and would probably have done it all without pay. But we also were delighted to share the greater understanding of these places that we came away with.

JULY 3, 1988

Walking the Chuckery

If trees could talk, a stately burr oak in the Chuckery area of Cascade Valley Park would have some three hundred years' worth of tales to tell. It would recall exactly how and when two of its branches were shaped to resemble two arms bent upward at the elbow, so that it became known as the Signal Tree. It would describe how the Cuyahoga River, along whose banks it once grew, drifted to a new course several hundred yards away. And it would, no doubt, offer insight about the area's transition from a peaceful valley in which generations of Indians hunted and fished to a highly traveled woodland only two miles from downtown Akron.

Even without the gift of speech, the Signal Tree continues to capture the imaginations of all who encounter it, just as it has since the earliest settlers arrived in the Western Reserve. Its story has been told many times in local histories and newspapers. We knew exactly where to find this oldest of area landmarks. What we didn't know was that the remarkable tree was surrounded by a remarkably pristine park—among the MetroParks system's newest.

The Peck Road entrance off Cuyahoga Street, just south of the Akron Corrections Facility, is easy to miss. Unlike the Oxbow area of the park just to the north, where baseball diamonds are clearly visible from the road, the Chuckery area shows no signs of development until one has traveled well beyond what's visible from Cuyahoga Street.

We began our walk at the second parking area. Our path, paved with a thick layer of woodchips, led us past lush growths of lavender and white wildflowers. We could hear the river racing unseen ahead of us, and we quickened our pace until we reached a clearing, where ten picnic tables and grills stood waiting to be occupied.

We picked up the Chuckery's 2.4-mile hiking trail at the arrowhead marker near the river bank and followed it back into the woods, first following the river, then veering away from the water and passing what appeared to be an oxbow filled in places with stagnant water.

As we moved away from the river, we began to hear a humming sound, which we correctly guessed to be the whine of tires against the steel grid of the high-level bridge connecting North Main Street in Akron with State Road in Cuyahoga Falls. The only other sounds were the occasional scolding of birds as we ventured into their domains and the rustling of animals in the brush near the trail.

Finally, we came to our destination, the grassy meadow dominated at its center by the Signal Tree. A split-rail fence about 170 feet in circumference surrounds the giant oak. Three benches just outside the circle provide the eye

A stately burr oak in Cascade Valley Park's Chuckery area is called the Signal Tree.

something by which to estimate the tree's size. And a large metal plaque dated 1986 tells the story we'd read so many times before: "Trees with unusual shapes were often used by Indians as landmarks to identify important trails. This three-hundred-year-old burr oak (*quereus macrocarpa*) marked the northernmost point of the portage trail, which connected the Cuyahoga (whose course was much closer to the tree) and the Tuscarawas Rivers."

We studied two freshly planted soccer fields on either side of the meadow and concluded that quiet time would soon be over in the park named for the woodchucks that were once its principal population.

JUNE 3, 1990

Earth Day at the Top O' the World

Watching the sunset at the Top O' the World is an unforgettable, almost spiritual experience that we hesitated to share. Standing on a grassy hillside in a park few people know about, one is tempted to keep it that way—to save the place for one's own. That was Chuck's feeling when he first took me to the 162-acre tract given to the Akron Metropolitan Park District in 1967 by the late E. Reginald and Rhea Adam, who so loved their summer home they wanted to preserve its vistas for all to enjoy. So we chose Earth Day 1990 to visit the Top O' the World Park on West Bath Road between Northampton and Akron-Peninsula roads in Cuyahoga Falls. It is part of the Hampton Hills MetroPark.

But watching the sun slip over the green horizon was only part of our reason for going public about this special Akron place. A rutted horseshoe-shaped drive takes motorists into and out of the park, which remains little changed since the Adams owned it. The 150-year-old house, vacant since 1967, is boarded up but appears to be otherwise in good shape. On one of my recent visits, a woman sat on the front porch watching the sunset while her companion strolled the grounds. A big red barn stands at the edge of a large pond a few hundred feet east of the house. From this vantage point, an army

The setting sun lights a path at Top O' the World Park.

of unseen frogs serenades the night after the birds have ended their daytime singing. Except for a sign marking the 3.2-mile Adam Run trail into the woods, this might still be the hilltop yard of a private residence.

Our path began as a tractor-wide swath cut through a meadow, which was mostly last season's tall brown grass. A six-foot-tall evergreen in the middle of the grass looked out of place. The real treats awaited in the woods. As the path turned to the west, we walked through branches covered with a velvet-like growth that, backlit by the sun, shimmered. If the place had been quiet before, it became even more so as we walked deeper into the forest over a pine-needle carpet. We passed a sign marking a 1968 Girl Scout tree planting, then headed into what can only be described as canyons, cut through the hills by several streams that run through the property. Ahead we saw the first of a series of wooden footbridges that carried the path across the water.

The quietest, loneliest place on our walk was a marshy lowland before the path started upward again. Wildflowers grew in abundance, and moss-covered logs were strewn everywhere, many with seashell-shaped fungus growing on the bark not layered with moss.

The woods were growing darker, so we started back, up a series of railroad-tie stairs set into the hillside on the path to the old Adam refuge and the two log benches that conveniently face the western horizon. It was there I sat nearly two years before, watching the sun set on the day of my brother's funeral. Chuck had shown me the Top O' the World Park just a few months earlier, and it seemed a fitting place to remember that last sunset Tony and I shared at La Jolla Cove in San Diego. He captured it on videotape, narrating the action as the burning orange ball disappeared into the Pacific Ocean. Staring across the green Cuyahoga Valley on Earth Day 1990, as I had on the day we buried Tony in All Saints Cemetery in Northfield Center, I could almost hear him saying, "Almost down. Almost down."

In Step with Nature

Seneca Pond feels so remote that when we stood at its edge, we felt like trespassers. The pond, one of two at the Akron Metropolitan Park District's Seiberling Naturealm, gives depth and scope to the expression "communing with nature." It is a place so quiet that one is moved to speak in whispers, as in a library or cathedral.

The whole idea at the Naturealm is to maintain a setting in which humankind is as unobtrusive as possible, and our vantage point at Seneca Pond worked to that end. It was a small clearing at the end of a short path through the woods. A carpet of wood chips, a low fence of moss-covered wood pilings on the pond side of the clearing, and a single bench beneath a canopy of wild crabapple trees were the only manmade intrusions.

Frogs sang to us from the thick growth of cattails along the water's edge, and we were reminded of a children's fable by the late Dr. Adib Karam, who likened the bristly spikes of cattails gone to seed to an ice-cream-cone garden.

From the bench, we could see the construction site of the Naturealm's underground visitor's center, which will open next year. The roof of the center is a grassy knoll with skylights that, when screened by shrubs, won't be visible to the public. As part of our tour, we got to stand atop the center, something the public won't get to do. The entrance will be planted with shrubs to give the effect of carrying the outside indoors, said our guide, Andy Kimmel, an administrative assistant. The lobby is paneled in wormy chestnut that was cut in the 1930s and stored for years by the park system.

From there, we began a tour of a series of connecting concrete domes that will house exhibits titled *Introduction to Nature*. The seasons will be depicted in an abstract indoor wood, its settings stylized so as not to compete with the outdoors. Visitors will also stroll through a meadow filled with living creatures, a marsh, and a birdwatching room. They'll pause at a set of windows overlooking Seneca Pond. At the bottom of a ramp, they'll be asked to imagine themselves frog-sized as they enter a tube surrounded by a simulated watery scene for a fish's-eye view of life.

A chrome-plated humanoid will stand at the entrance to an exhibit on man's influence on nature. Rats, toxic waste, and endangered species will be among the displays. Visitors will get a more optimistic view of the world at the next exhibit, which will show returning species as pieces of a puzzle being put together, and at a photomural titled *The Future is in Your Hands.* The last exhibit before the lobby will be a small alcove at another window through which the animals can watch the people watching them with binoculars.

The center is being built around exhibits designed by Jean Jacques Andre of British Columbia, who has earned a reputation worldwide, said Metro-Parks Superintendent John Daily. It was designed by Gayle Scafe, president of Terra-Dome Systems Incorporated of Independence, Missouri, and it will also feature a classroom and laboratory offering area schoolchildren hands-on experience and an auditorium that will seat up to one hundred. Ground was broken in the fall of 1989. The new building will replace the one-story brick center, which was built as a ranch-style home and has been used by the park system since 1965. This will be razed, in keeping with the goal of unobtrusiveness. Kimmel called the new center "Bert's dream come true," referring to MetroParks chief naturalist Bert Szabo (now retired).

We had spent an hour hardly looking at nature, so we thanked Kimmel for the tour, shifted gears, and took to the paths. There were three to choose from—the .2-mile Arboretum, the 1.1-mile Seneca, and the half-mile Cherry Lane. We took the last, which sloped and curved and at one point grew wide enough for the passage of two cars but in most places remained a footpath just wide enough for two or three walkers.

One of the first of many signs we encountered suggested conversations be kept at low volume in deference to others using the park. Another sign matter-of-factly announced the presence of poison ivy along the path's edge. Perhaps the most poetic described an old plow coulter: "This tool sliced the sod so the plow could till the soil. Now it rusts away as the invading forest enriches the soil with rotting leaves." A glacial boulder, a six-by-five-foot piece of granite, stood among the trees, many of which were labeled.

A sign on one tree posed a trick question: A label on a tree is nine feet from the ground. If the tree grows a foot a year, how long will it take for the label to be twelve feet from the ground?

Answer: The tree grows up from the top, so the label won't move up.

We discovered a suspension bridge in the middle of the forest. We might have missed it because it was along the .45-mile Fernwood Loop, a branch of Cherry Lane, and we didn't want to deviate from the path. But curiosity won out, and we were rewarded with a spectacular view of what a sign described as "a typical ravine of Sand Run. . . . The ridges are dry and support oaks and hickories, while the ravines are moist and you find maples and beeches." From the center of the bridge, we could see the stream quietly zigzagging below. Just beyond the Fernwood Loop, Cherry Lane began an upward climb that is not for the out-of-shape stroller; then it took us out of the woods and back to the path leading to the visitor's center.

While we were concentrating on the flora, the animals were eyeing us. A raccoon studied Chuck as he drew, and I came under the scrutiny of a family of rabbits eating clover near the construction site. Our last stop was the rock-and-herb garden, which filled the air with wonderful scents. Leeks displayed grapefruit-size seed blossoms, and butterflies fluttered amid the oregano plants. Here we encountered more baby bunnies, which ignored us as they munched their way back to their nests.

A sundial read 5 o'clock, which was incorrect even allowing for the difference between standard and daylight savings time. Right after we noted this, we came upon a planting of sage, suggesting a title, perhaps for a rock group: Five O'Clock Shadow and Riders of the Purple Sage.

SEPTEMBER 3, 1989

Walking into the Past

Fairlawn Mayor Peter Kostoff invited us to go walking in the proposed Fort Island Park. We got a history lesson about life in the Copley Swamp in the 1650s, taught by the mayor and Janet Monroe, principal of Fort Island School. Their classroom was an Indian mound near Trunko Road and Interstate 77.

Kostoff brought a map of the area adjacent to Griffith Park, where he and Monroe briefed us before we ventured into the mosquito-infested marsh. The map showed yet-to-be-built hiking trails and boardwalks meandering through Fort Island Park, which will someday link Griffith, the school, and Fort Island and Beech Mounds, where legend has it that the Erie Indians made their last stand against the Iroquois more than one hundred years before the American Revolution.

Our trail to the mound area was practically nonexistent, but we entered the marsh near a thick-trunked and wonderfully gnarled tree at the cul-de-sac of Erie Drive. This was the way University of Akron archaeologists had come last spring when they test excavated the mounds for evidence of prehistoric habitation.

Fort Island Mound is so-called because it rises well above surrounding land; it was probably once surrounded seasonally by water, and in legend it was a fortification. Nearby is Beech Mound, named for trees that grow there and are thought to have been used for defense by the Erie from around 1200 to the 1650s. A third mound, called Sugar, disappeared when Interstate 77 blazed its way through Fairlawn.

As we approached Fort Island Mound, a loud cracking sound stopped us in our tracks as a thirty-foot section of a tall dead tree collapsed and fell to the ground about twenty feet in front of us. We all stared, speechless for a moment, then laughed at what we had witnessed. "Would there have been a sound had we not been there?" I wondered. "Yes," Monroe said with conviction.

Chuck spotted an ancient tree, hollow at its base, that could have been home to one of J.R.R. Tolkien's hobbits. We stopped to examine a large, fungus-covered fallen tree with massive roots exposed.

"I've been using it for science lessons for fifteen years," Monroe said.

For three of those years, she was assisted by Robert Imars, a retiree who donned Indian garb and paint to become Chief Eager Beaver on field trips.

"He came to me and volunteered to teach," Monroe said. "We worked out a curriculum for all grade levels."

Together, they walked in the footsteps of the Erie with more than a thousand students and adults before Imars died in July. Kostoff gave the eulogy at his funeral. Imars was among the residents who spearheaded the formation of the Fairlawn Archives and Historical Commission.

Fort Island has been on the National Register of Historic Places since 1970, but plans for its development lay dormant for more than fifteen years. During the last two years, the city has acquired parcels that will link the school, Griffith Park, and the mounds into a forty-three-acre park. Clearly, it requires people of vision to see what the area was and what it might be. At a glance, with I-77 traffic roaring by a few yards away, it might be dismissed as a wet lowland with a couple of wooded hills.

NOVEMBER 6, 1991

A Legend Revisited

The morning mist was just beginning to lift when we arrived at the footbridge over Schocalog Run. The sun was low in the east, and the moon was still clearly visible in the western sky over Fort Island and Griffith parks in Fairlawn. A blue heron waded a few feet away. It stood statuelike, apparently afraid, waiting for the human visitors to move on. This section of the larger Copley Swamp belongs to the flora and fauna, thanks to the City of Fairlawn and an Ohio Humanities Council grant, which created the Fort Island Interpretive Project.

We came to explore more than two miles of new boardwalk and trails a few weeks before the public got its first look at them. To learn about the new park, we first had to understand what it wasn't. Two years ago, we heard the legend of Fort Island, where a small band of Erie Indians was said to have made its last stand against the Iroquois in the 1650s. But it didn't happen that way, say scholars who have spent three years studying the area. The Erie-Iroquois battle took place somewhere between what is now Erie, Pennsylvania, and Buffalo, New York, in 1654–56, historians now say. The Erie never lived in Northeast Ohio.

The legend is an important part of the area's oral history, says University of Akron anthropologist Lynn Metzger. It was the rallying point in the community's effort to get Fort Island on the National Register of Historic Places in 1970 and saved it from being eradicated by Interstate 77, which today forms a protective border to the nature center. A series of signs will explain what visitors will be looking at along the boardwalk and trails.

Our guided tour included Glenn Frank, a retired Kent State University geology professor; his wife, Betty; Forest Smith, who teaches anthropology and biology at UA's Wayne College in Orrville; landscape architect Greg Fox; and Metzger. They, along with historian George Knepper, UA archaeologist Elizabeth Mancz, and UA nutrition and family ecologist Victoria Wade, formed a Fort Island study committee. There was so much to see that Chuck and I returned a few days later for a second look.

While the facts disprove the old Erie legend, they do reveal what the scholars consider more exciting evidence about the area. The Fort Island Mound, thought to have been an Indian fortress, is a kame, a geological formation produced by successive advances and retreats of glacial ice. The terrace surrounding it was produced by wave action during an ancient period when the mound was surrounded by a lake.

Woodland people hunted, foraged, and grew crops in and near the swamp from 1000 to 1650. Archaeological study produced evidence of a palisade of woven slender poles along the ditch surrounding Fort Island. Palisades were used to define space. This mound with the archaeological evidence of the pal-

Paths run by the mound at Fort Island Park.

isade is similar to others found in Ohio and Northern Kentucky that are believed to be prehistoric ceremonial sites.

Volunteers have built a replica of the fence, which can be seen along the gravel trail that leads from the boardwalk to the mound. The boardwalk over the peat bog was still under construction the day of our tour. Because the summer was so dry, the normally moist peat was dry and cracked. Our guides pointed out a clearing near where the boardwalk parallels Bancroft Road. Here, they said, a bulldozer sank three feet into the peat and had to be pulled out. Frank's study indicates the peat is around forty feet deep there and rests on quartz sand left by the glacier.

Poison ivy virtually covered one tall tree along the path. Also plentiful was jewelweed, which our guides said relieves the itch of poison ivy when applied to infected areas; sumac, poisonous and non-; and plants with such names as meadowsweet, blackhaw, and virgin's bower.

Wild rice, duck potatoes, cranberries, and blueberries, grown in the area called the aging bog, fed the prehistoric inhabitants, as did game they hunted—everything from deer to woolly mammoths. A bushy-tailed squirrel darting out from under the boardwalk gave us such a start that it might just as well have been a mammoth. Less menacing were the chipmunks and groundhogs we caught glimpses of. Overhead, a family of yellow finches flew from tree to tree.

The entrance to the park is on Trunko Road off Bancroft Road in Fairlawn.

JANUARY 6, 1991

What a View!

If James A. Michener were to write a book about Brandywine Falls in Sagamore Hills, he probably would take a long-term lease at the 152-year-old bed-and-breakfast operated by Katie and George Hoy and make it his headquarters while he did extensive research on the formation of the sedimentary rocks over which Brandywine Creek falls. In the megabook he would no doubt produce, the author would likely include a few paragraphs on the Ice Age glacier that left its imprint on what would become the Western Reserve, and certainly a chapter on the river that gave the Cuyahoga Valley National Recreation Area its name.

Chuck and I explored Brandywine Falls on a warm and sunny Thursday before the season's first real snowfall. We began at the picnic tables in a small stand of trees bordering the parking lot. A sign at Stanford Road, just before the bridge that carries Brandywine Road over Interstate 271, marks the entrance to the lot, which, along with public restrooms and the winding wooden deck that leads to observation platforms, are all part of improvements completed by the park service during the past year to make the falls more accessible to the public.

Chuck marveled at how different the place looked at this time of year, when the trees were bare. When he visited the falls for the first time in August, the full foliage hid the observation deck and muffled the sound of the falling water. Now the water competed with the motor sounds from the freeway and crunching leaves as we hiked across Stanford to the deck.

Soon we were on the seven-foot-wide wooden walkway. The first section is crescent-shaped and at first takes visitors away from the falls. Terrain may have dictated this course, but I couldn't help but wonder if some other logic had been employed. The path drew our attention to trees and hills that we might have ignored in a beeline trip to the falls and back.

Along the winding walkway, which hugged the rocky contour of the gorge, we found the views improving with every step. I scribbled a description, one word I've always hesitated to use in writing: Breathtaking. It really applies here.

First there was the tree. In a forest filled with trees that probably took root within the last twenty years stands the carcass of one that shaded our grandfathers, and perhaps theirs as well. There are no markers to tell us when it died, but it was left undisturbed by the engineers at the first curve of the deck. Though many of the tree's limbs have fallen, one thick branch seemingly defies gravity. It has been all but severed from the trunk, but it remains in place, suspended in the crook of another younger tree. We hadn't yet seen the tree's other—hollowed—side. Beyond this grand old tree, the hill plunged down to the creek, which meandered through the canyon away from our destination.

We moved on, rounding the crescent to a fork in the path, where we elected to take the lower deck first. A sign warned us that this section would be closed when icy conditions prevailed. There are five sets of stairs—sixty-five steps in all—as the deck leads visitors to the lower observation platform.

Looking up at the underside of sediments originally laid down in some kind of water, we were able to see and touch thin-stemmed mushrooms and other fungi and ferns and the webs of countless spiders. And we dodged the dripping water that in time will take its toll upon the wooden walkway.

There's a resting place just before the last set of stairs. Above it, a tree grows down from the hill, before its trunk curves upwards at an angle of forty-five degrees. The tree is about twenty feet high from root to tip, and we wondered how long it would grow before gravity or man brought it down.

While we admired the tree, a mother with three young children marched by on their way to the observation platform, where she posed them on a bench and began taking their pictures, using all the coaxing expressions and sounds associated with children's photographers.

The falls, our reason for being there, we all but ignored during most of our visit. We walked most of the way looking away from the falls, looking instead at the walls against which the lower walkway was built, at the puddles and drips. And yet the falls are truly spectacular—another word I seldom use—even when the creek is but a trickle in dry weather. When the light is right—and it was when we were there—the sun casts a shadow of the falling water against the north wall of the gorge, which is green with moss and red from the iron-rich rock.

It was lunchtime, and more people began to arrive. A couple sat in the sun at one of the picnic tables on the north side of the gorge near the inn. A well-dressed elderly couple and a young man with a legal pad passed us as we head-

Trees grow below and along the Brandywine Falls walkway.

ed back. The place has become so popular as a setting for wedding photos that bridal parties sometimes block the path for other visitors.

We found that the serpentine pattern of the deck is etched in blue, green, and yellow into the top rail of the overlook at the east end of the upper deck, just before the last section of wooden walkway leading to the ruins of the old Brandywine Mill. From the mill's foundation, one can look down on the falls from the safe side of an iron railing. Warnings of the dangers on the other side are printed in English, German, French, Spanish, and Japanese. More dramatic is the warning of the water itself as it runs rapidly beneath the Brandywine Road bridge, slows into a pool, and then speeds off again to cascade over the falls in two branches.

AUGUST 4, 1991

A Study in Green

Today's adventure is being brought to you by the color green. Make that *colors* green. Have you ever noticed how many varieties of green there are in nature? We did, along a mile or so of the walking and jogging trail of Akron's Sand Run MetroPark. For more than an hour on a hot, muggy morning, we paused frequently to study the roof of green that cooled the path in shades that ranged from almost black in the shadows to almost white where sunlight broke through. In between were greens tinged blue, yellow, and gray.

Another thing we noticed about this urban park is that one is seldom alone. And at times there were virtual pedestrian traffic jams. The experience brought to mind Chaucer's *Canterbury Tales*. One could pick a spot and watch the world—or at least a fair representation of Akron—come by. The first people we saw were two members of the park maintenance crew cleaning up. Within sixty seconds of our arrival, we saw three people walking four dogs, so I decided to keep count. We saw only two more dogs during our visit. And no dog droppings, I'm happy to report.

The parade included walkers and joggers of every size, shape, and age, in-

Bikers and hikers fill the trail at Sand Run Park.

cluding babies pushed in strollers. One woman, as she passed, held her index finger to her lips in the universal call for silence. Most of the people greeted us. Some, including groups of youngsters led on hikes by adults, we heard before we saw. It was my first visit to the path, but Chuck regularly walks there. He said the crowd we encountered would be replaced at lunchtime by another group out for an hour's exercise, and that one would be replaced by the after-five walkers and joggers. We encountered some wildlife along the way. Chipmunks scurried across our path, startling us, although, judging by the way they ran, they were more frightened than we were.

Our footfalls created a moderate tempo along a path softened by long brown pine needles. Birds were joyously loud, all but drowning out the sound of traffic along the parkway that parallels the footpath. Through the trees to the north we could see backyards, but unless one searches for them, they are easily overlooked.

Chuck pointed out the place where the path runs along the edge of a picnic area and recalled stopping there at sunset to study the moon shortly after Neil Armstrong and the Eagle landed in 1969. The place remains among his favorites.

While we talked, we heard the scolding of a bird and looked up through the trees to see a small bird chasing a hawk—apparently away from its nest. Wild grape plants growing along the path had leaves that looked like lace because of something that was eating them. Slightly beyond the Wadsworth picnic area, the path runs along a marsh that is the only separation from the backyards. At least one path leads from the residential neighborhood to the park, and conceivably some of the people we shared the trail with live nearby.

Climbing a slight rise, we could see the railroad tracks on which the new Cuyahoga Valley Scenic Railroad runs from Cleveland to Akron. We also could see the traffic along Riverview Road a short distance away. As we approached the park maintenance area, we crossed a bridge over a lush area filled with ferns and wild plants I've always called elephant ears. Something growing gave off a pleasant fragrance that we couldn't identify. Leafy vines covered the trunks of thick trees fifteen feet or higher. Initials and names were carved in the surface of a smooth-barked tree: "Cindy," "the class of '75," "Evie."

We came to a waterfall near a shelter called Mingo. The path doglegged across a bridge over the small stream, practically a trickle. It dropped less than six feet, but recorded on tape, the falling water sounded more like a river.

A baby raccoon walked along the bank of the creek about fifty yards upstream from the waterfall. Two women coming toward us on the path said the animal had come up to them, apparently lost, and they expressed concern that it would die. We suggested they report it to a park ranger.

Orange daylilies grew in abundance along the path, and through the trees we spotted what looked like a totem pole. It was a thick-trunked dead tree with an orange cast and a sculpted look. Nearby, we encountered a recently fallen tree, perhaps downed by lightning. We could trace the course of its fall across the path by the scars and broken limbs on neighboring trees. It had been cut up on the spot and its sections left on either side of the path—three pieces on the north side, three more on the south side just off the path, and the rest down a ravine. Other downed trees had been there longer. The roots of one looked like an extracted tooth. Another was covered with a thick carpet of moss.

We came to another bridge and a second waterfall. This one wasn't as loud as the first. Around another bend, we came to the place where the road fords Sand Run and stepping-stones carry walkers across the stream.

As we neared the end of our walk, we were scolded by a couple of crows perched on branches a few feet above our heads. We discovered the reason for their angst as they scurried away a few feet down the path. It was a baby crow that apparently had fallen from its nest. It was unhurt but unable to achieve lift-off.

Perhaps the day's biggest treat was the appearance of a flying insect the likes of which I had never seen before. It was about the size of a dragonfly and rested on a leafy plant at the edge of the path. Chuck recognized it to be a damselfly. Its color? An iridescent blue-green.

Close Encounters of the Bird Kind

Remember that scene in Walt Disney's *Snow White and the Seven Dwarfs* in which all the gentle beasts of the forest prance and swarm around Snow White as she wanders down a woodland trail? Wasn't it a bluebird that landed on her finger and joined her in a duet? We weren't singing or even bird-watching when we arrived at Firestone MetroPark, but we encountered a scene reminiscent of the 1939 animated cartoon classic on a hiking trail along the Tuscarawas Race, just north of East Warner Road in that section of Akron that juts into Coventry Township.

We came to see the popular sledding hill and the Coventry Oaks pavilion, which is nearing completion. We spotted the pavilion from South Main Street just before we turned east on Warner, but found no signs telling us how to get to the new structure when we arrived at the parking lot closest to the hillside.

A trail from the Warner Road lot took us over a footbridge spanning the race, then forked to the left—northwest—along the canal-like stream and to the right—northeast—toward the Tuscarawas Meadows shelter, which the new pavilion is replacing. We opted for the right, hoping to find some person or sign to guide us to the new pavilion, and crossed a second bridge that arched above the Tuscarawas River just east of the dam at Harrington Road. The shelter was deserted, but another hiker pointed us back the way we had just come, saying the trail along the race would take us to our destination.

The birds seemed to be waiting. Four chickadees were literally flying in our faces, zooming in close, then retreating to low-hanging branches of trees that line the trail. Two cardinals landed at our feet and chattered, as if to say, "Where's the food?" Tame or brazen? Maybe a little of both, we decided, as we continued along the trail escorted by our winged friends.

The last of a recent snowfall hugged the corrugated steel that reinforces the northern bank of the race, and trees on the opposite bank were reflected

Birds abounded at Firestone MetroPark.

in the water, which was still except for the wake of three ducks and five drakes that swam noisily in our direction. The hikers must be generous, we concluded, and agreed not to come empty-handed on our next visit.

Through the trees we spotted the top of the hill, which was empty of sledders on the weekday morning we visited, and a Goodyear blimp, droning across the sky.

The chickadees persisted in their up-close-and-personal inspection and, as Chuck pointed out another cardinal in a tree across the race, one of them made like a dive-bomber for his outstretched hand, hovering for a moment before veering away. Shushing Chuck, I played a statue—arm extended, palm up—and watched the chickadees swarm around us like bees around a sweet treat. One of the birds, no larger than a hen's egg, landed on my hand. It clutched my index finger and pecked lightly at the fabric of my glove, then just sat there for at least ten seconds before rejoining the swarm.

Our ornithological inventory for the day was quite impressive—titmice, white-bellied juncos, blue jays, nuthatches, a red-bellied woodpecker, a downy woodpecker, a flock of geese flying in V-formation, a soaring hawk, and a lone seagull—but for me, everything else we did was anticlimax.

The trail veered away from the race as we drew near the pavilion and there was no path from the trail to the new structure, so we hiked uphill across a section of recently graded, unsodded soil that was, thankfully, frozen. The building is sided in wood painted a pale cherry and gray with brown stone. Peering through the front doors on the north side, we could see the sledding hill through the floor-to-ceiling rear windows. A sign on the door warned us to stay out while the floors were being sealed—an activity we witnessed when we walked around to a patio on the building's south side.

We crossed the race on a decorative poured-concrete bridge, then trudged up the snow-covered hill to find a lone log bench and a magnificent view of the Akron skyline. We were able to identify such landmarks as the apartment tower at East Avenue and Manchester Road, the Bridgestone-Firestone and former B. F. Goodrich complexes, the Canal Park YMCA, 1 Cascade Plaza, the First National Tower, a checkered water tower on Arlington Street, and the Airdock.

It was from the hilltop that we saw the geese, the hawk, and the gull.

JUNE 4, 1995

The End of Spring

Remember all the don'ts of childhood?
Don't touch.
Don't tease.
Don't interrupt.
Don't talk to strangers.
Don't wake the baby.
Don't stay up too late.
Don't gulp your food.
Don't eat the last cookie.
Don't forget to brush.
Don't forget to call.
Don't cut across the neighbor's lawn.
Don't get your shoes muddy.
Don't splash in the puddles.

Remember the glee with which dancer Gene Kelly did just that in the film classic *Singin' in the Rain?*

Is it any wonder that two grown men would take such delight in walking in the rain? That was our simple premise: Sharing the experience of strolling around Akron's Highland Square area on one of the rainiest days of the season.

Walking in the rain has always been a treat for me, as long as I am dressed for it and the downpour isn't accompanied by lightning and thunder. It probably started as a childish delight at defying the grown-ups' rules, much like staying up all night, but as I grew older I experienced a genuine cleansing feeling, not personally, but as if I were watching the world going through a giant car wash.

Chuck picked our destination, Shady Park, a tiny grassy triangle bounded by West Market Street, South Rose Boulevard, and Metlin Avenue, and maintained by the city of Akron. As parks go, Shady Park offers little more than its name suggests—trees to shield you from the sun and a single bench. Of course, the sun was safely hidden behind a solid bank of weeping gray clouds when we popped open our umbrellas and set out from Ayers's studio near Portage Path Elementary School on South Portage Path. Our route took us along Elmore, Corson, Ardmore, and Everett Avenues to Rose and the park.

The trunks of trees were blackened on the sides exposed to the wind and rain, and dry and shades lighter on the sheltered sides. We needed no calendar to tell us that spring was on the wane. Azalea and rhododendron blossoms were splattered on the ground beneath their bushes, and the sidewalks were carpeted with thousands of wing-shaped maple seeds. My childhood friends and I called these seeds "helicopters" because of the way they twirled as they floated to earth from the branches or, once landed, from our upraised hands. Wet maple seeds aren't much fun to play with, so we concentrated on the lush scene as viewed through the steady but gentle rain.

All but a couple of homes we saw along the way were attractive and well-maintained. It was an ordinary weekday, yet the Stars and Stripes were flying at several homes. Yards appeared to be routinely well-tended, with a few showing the results of years of careful planting and pruning.

Everett Avenue stands out in a neighborhood filled with streets paved with red bricks. Everett is paved with pale yellow bricks that appear to be older than the red. Yellow and red, the streets gleamed as if covered with shellac, reminding us how slippery wet brick can be for motorists. The sidewalk at the corner of Everett and Marvin Avenues has the street names engraved in the pavement. The word "avenue" is abbreviated two different ways—"AV" and "AVE."

All sidewalks lead to Shady Park.

We arrived at the park where Everett ends at Rose, and from that side of the triangle Chuck found two illustration subjects, the bench and a chestnut tree heavy with ivory-colored blossoms. The tree and the rain reminded me of an old pop standard that begins "April in Paris, chestnuts in blossom . . ." This was Akron at the end of May, but the scene captured the mood of the song. The bench holds a special place in Chuck's memory, as does the park. He had been suggesting it as a locale for one of our walks since last fall because, like so many of the places we have visited since this series began, it was a familiar place just waiting to be discovered. I knew he was right as soon as we got there. I had driven by the park countless times without noticing it.

The park was more familiar to him because he lives in the neighborhood and has walked to and around it more times than he can remember, pushing his daughter and later his son in a stroller. On one trip, he left the stroller at home and carried his son, who was not yet walking, and thought his arms would drop off from the weight of the sleeping child. He saw the bench as he approached the park like a thirsty wanderer approaching an oasis in the desert.

Looking across the park, Chuck selected an angle that would best show the bench, the trunk of the tree that shades it, and two of the three stone columns at the entrance to Mayfield Avenue across Market Street. He also confessed that he had never noticed there were three columns until that moment. We walked all three sides of the triangle, pausing to admire a home in a former church at the point where Metlin and Mull Avenues come together at Market. Its cornerstone is inscribed "St. Saviour Chapel & Parish House 1909."

Chuck found the vantage point for his main illustration at the corner of Rose and Market, where the glistening sidewalks stretched on in two directions, seemingly to infinity. The geometric pattern drew his eye. To me, it was a reminder of the sidewalks that were our playgrounds years ago in Cleveland, where I learned never to step on a crack, lest I break my mother's back.

As we headed east along Market toward the business strip and our luncheon destination, Dodie's restaurant, a car stopped and a woman passenger rolled down the window and asked if we knew how to get to the Tangier restaurant.

"You're heading for it," Chuck said, while I suppressed my laughter. "Look for the big blue onion dome."

The joke?

None, really, but each of our walks seems to include a link to an earlier one. The onion dome, which dominated Chuck's illustration for the first walk in March 1987, has shown up in several others.

For the record, we were dressed properly but were still wet nearly to our knees and, even though we had umbrellas, on the shoulders of our jackets.

It was worth it.

JULY 4, 1999

Tiny Park and a Grand Old Flag

If you head downtown along West Market Street on this Fourth of July, you'll likely see a huge American flag dominating the sky above one of Akron's oldest and smallest parks. The view is an optical illusion because the thirty-by-fifty-foot flag doesn't really fly over the triangle formed by Market, Valley, and North Streets. The Stars and Stripes adorn the top of a pole at VanDevere Olds' used-car lot a few doors to the east at 301 West Market. But the flag is a big enough illusion that we were inspired to take a closer look.

Actually, we visited Alexander Park several times, looking for the best angle from which to view it, and collected some historical details along the way. In the end, Chuck picked the view from the northeast tip of the triangle at North and Valley for his illustration. This perspective shows the park against a background that features two American flags, flying at McDonald's, 390 West Market, and at the colonial-style building next door at 400 West Market.

Chuck's reasons for selecting that view were aesthetic. I concurred on historical grounds, after reading a couple of stories by the late Margot Jackson in the *Akron Beacon Journal* archives. The pancake-flat site of the restaurant and office buildings used to be an estate called Forest Hill, Jackson wrote in 1986. The subject of her story was J. Park Alexander, who bought the land in 1860 and built a twenty-room home at the highest point of the property. Alexander developed a fire-resistant brick, which earned him his fortune. His principal business was the Diamond Fire Brick Company, but he also operated a couple of oil refineries, which he eventually sold to John D. Rockefeller in the early days of the Standard Oil Company. Alexander also served on the Akron City Council and in the Ohio legislature and was an early member of the Summit County Agricultural Society.

The triangle across from Forest Hill was known as Neptune Park during Alexander's lifetime. It had a fountain and was the scene of summer band concerts. Alexander died in 1908, and within ten years the park was renamed in his memory. Later still, the house and the hill were leveled for the Dutch Folk Chevrolet dealership. Today three signs are displayed on the triangle, but none names the park. One sign marks it as a spot entrusted to the care of Keep Akron Beautiful, and the products of members' labors were in full bloom to prove it. The other signs herald the summer arts festival at Hardesty Park.

We walked each side of the triangle, then climbed six well-worn sandstone steps and cut across the park along a path other feet have worn in the turf. Shrubs that border the flowerbeds glistened with droplets from the park's underground sprinkler system, and we noticed the lawn was bright green along the edges of the beds, but otherwise brown from the recent dry spell.

An elderly man crossed the park along the same path we had taken, nodded a greeting, and sat on the bench on the Market side of the park. We guessed he was waiting for the next Metro bus, but we were wrong. After a couple of minutes' rest, he crossed Market and went into the restaurant, emerging a few minutes later with a coffee and a copy of the *Beacon Journal*.

It took a phone call to the Olds dealership to answer one nagging question after our walk. Why, we wondered, does the dealer sometimes fly the huge flag and at other times a much smaller one? General Manager Vince

Paris explained that a storm will rip a thirty-by-fifty-foot flag to shreds, so he hoists a fifteen-by-twenty-five-foot flag when bad weather is predicted.

"But the big flag will be flying for the Fourth of July, rain or shine," Paris said.

AKRON CITY MAGAZINE
JANUARY–APRIL 2003

Alexander Park Revisited

A message scribbled on a postcard nearly one hundred years ago described Akron's Alexander Park—then called Neptune Park—as "a dandy place to spend a summer evening." The writer was referring to band concerts and other events at the triangle at West Market, North, and Valley Streets, which was the first parcel the city of Akron purchased exclusively for use as a park. That was in 1880, for the sum of $1,200.

We didn't know these facts when we first visited the park in 1999. Revisiting it four years later, we admired its restoration, which was completed in July with installation of the new sixteen-foot fountain, a replica of one that stood in the park until the late 1920s. Keep Akron Beautiful and the city of Akron, partners in the restoration, were helped by private donations, largest of which was $15,000 from the Akron Garden Club.

The original fountain—given to the city by J. Park Alexander—had carvings of the Greek god Neptune around its base. These, we learned, are to be added to the custom-built cast aluminum replica. The carvings gave the park its original name, which was spelled out in decorative iron above the entrance when Alexander lived across West Market.

Chuck's illustration showcased the new fountain, the park's curved brick walkways, and the car dealer's huge flag. The Stars and Stripes went well with Keep Akron Beautiful's new Liberty Garden on the park's north side. The garden's red, white, and blue floral beds surround a plaque that commemorates the victims and the brave of September 11, 2001, and celebrates liberty.

CHAPTER SEVEN

Exploring
the Towpath Trail

*By 1990, local attention turned to the rediscovery of an important historic regional re-
source, the Ohio & Erie Canal. The big ditch, as many called the canal, had opened the
region to the outside world in 1825, enabling the Akron area to become a bustling commercial center. Chuck and I began our examination of what remains of that historic era
at the amazing Mustill Store and returned in 2003 to marvel at what had transpired in
the thirteen intervening years. It was our eighth visit to the trail, which we visited in
each season, on our own and with knowledgeable guides.*

MAY 6, 1990

Rediscovering the Towpath

"Amazing" best describes the 162-year-old wood frame building at 248
Ferndale Street, just north of downtown Akron. The most amazing thing
about it and the only slightly newer house next door is that the buildings are
still standing and are in reasonably good condition. Ferndale is little more than
two wheel ruts running parallel to the Ohio & Erie Canal and north off North

Street a few paces west of Howard Street. Frederick Mustill operated a general store at Lock 15 until the flood of March 1913 put the canal out of business for good. The house and store are clearly visible from North to passing motorists. Yet few people we asked before and after our walk along the canal north of downtown had ever heard of Mustill's Store, much less visited it.

Among these few were Virginia Wojno-Forney of Akron and Tom Germain of Stow, members of the Cascade Locks Park Association task force. They donned their hiking gear and were our guides on our introductory visit. We began at the store, a two-story Greek revival structure that dates to 1828, according to the Akron Planning and Development Department. That's a year after the canal opened between Akron and Cleveland. The store, originally a cigar-box factory, stands on the west side of Ferndale. Lock 15 and its roaring canal waters are on the east side of the road. The building appears much as it did in photos taken before the flood, except for a front porch and an addition on the north side of the building, which are long gone. If the building ever wore any paint, it didn't show in photos dating to the 1860s and 1870s. Yet the wood siding apparently has weathered well.

Shutters believed to be original equipment protect front windows on the ground floor. Beneath them are panes of old, wavy window glass, according to Wojno-Forney. Metal and plywood cover most of the other windows. One front window on the second floor is broken, but the building looks otherwise unmolested. An outhouse stands on the north side of the store. The site is marked by a modern street lamp and an Ohio Edison meter.

Just south of the store and set back farther from Ferndale is the old lock-tender's Greek revival home, said to have been built shortly after the store. It appears well maintained. Sheets of plywood protect its windows and entrances. A roadside mailbox stands near a crumbling stone wall that marks its front property line. This was the home of Pete and Julia Ramnytz from 1955 until early 1989, when they sold it and the store to the city of Akron for $40,000. The purchase coincided with the birth of the Cascade Locks task force, whose members see the property as a key link in the recreational redevelopment of the canal towpath from Cleveland to Zoar.

This is how Frederick Mustill's house and store looked in 1990.

On this day, we concerned ourselves with one mile of the canal in downtown Akron. There were forty-four locks between Summit Lake, elevation 978 feet, its highest point, and Lake Erie, elevation 575 feet. In the mile between Lock 1, just south of Exchange Street and west of Main Street, and Lock 15, at Mustill Store, there were fifteen locks. The 1913 flood washed away the canal immediately north of Lock 15, so that its water merges with that of the Little Cuyahoga River at a point where a large sewer pipe, broken in one place, crosses the river.

Ferndale continues along a one-car-wide path for a few hundred feet, then more or less disappears into the brush just north of the lock. Gone are signs of residences that once stood along the street, houses that show up in pre-flood photos. Homes on higher ground to the west are visible through the trees.

Looking east from a vantage point along the rusting steel guardrail at the top of the lock, we could see the All-America and Expressway bridges carrying traffic to and from downtown Akron. Looking south, we could see the railroad trestle that carries the Cuyahoga Valley Line over the canal. Overhead, Ohio Edison power lines and jet vapor trails crisscrossed the sky, completing a picture that embraced virtually every aspect of the area's transportation story from the 1820s to the present. The view of the lock from the top, about thirty-five feet above, is of rushing water falling about ten feet at the south entrance to the lock and another three feet into the river.

For the rest of the morning and part of another on a second visit, we tramped through the brush south of North Street, along railroad tracks and trestles, around the Ace Rubber plant and behind the old Ohio Edison Beech Street power plant just north of the Innerbelt. We were seeking glimpses of Locks 14 through 11. Looking south from the North Street bridge over the canal, we saw Locks 14 and 13, which are close together and occur at a sharp bend in the canal.

There is no path along the canal, so we had to make our own along the east bank. It was early enough in the season that the foliage hadn't made it impenetrable. Wojno-Forney said this area will be part of a public biking and hiking trail leading from the Cuyahoga Valley National Recreation Area to downtown Akron, if the long-range goals of the task force are ever met.

She is bolstered in her hopes by the makeup of the task force, whose forty-two members include John Debo, national park director and a proponent of the Cleveland-to-Zoar corridor proposal; Akron deputy mayor James Phelps; Akron planning director James Alkire; Ward Three Councilman Marco Sommerville; Ace Rubber president Charles Snyder; and John Seiberling, whose legislation in the U.S. House of Representatives helped create the national park. Seiberling heads the government liaison committee. Debo and John Daily, Akron MetroParks director, serve with Wojno-Forney and others on the task force's long-range planning committee, which Germain heads. Just a year before, several members of Progress Through Preservation and other interested people hacked their way through the same brush for a similar look at the locks. The task force grew from this gathering.

To get to the tracks south of North Street, we cut across an overgrown parcel on the canal's west bank. Along the way, we discovered an old sandstone foundation. Upon closer examination back at the sidewalk along North, we recognized the remains of the sandstone steps leading to the home site. We headed east along the tracks—past an old frame and brick building that might have been a smokehouse—and we paused on the steel-bedded trestle over the canal. Looking back toward Lock 15, we could see Mustill Store and the locktender's house nestled against a background of trees, with Howard Street rising to the top of the hill toward St. Thomas Medical Center. Looking south, we could see Locks 13 and 12, Ace Rubber, the stacks of the Beech Street plant, the First National tower, and the tops of the floodlights at St. Vincent-St. Mary High School stadium.

At the end of the trestle, we found ourselves at the Furnace Street railhead, where Cuyahoga Valley Line passengers board and depart the excursion trains. A spur took us over another steel bridge leading nowhere. That is, one set of old tracks started south, then ended abruptly at the parking lot of an old yellow brick building on the west side of Howard Street, and another continued west into the brush. A tethered doberman standing guard in the parking lot ended any thought of venturing further. An old blue kitchen chair stood in the middle of the bridge, suggesting that the spot might be a popular vantage point for neighborhood children too short to see over the side.

Back over the trestle, we walked the tracks to North and Walnut Streets, then detoured south along Walnut before heading back to Mustill Store and our cars. Walnut runs south up a hill before it dead-ends at a second set of railroad tracks which span the valley on a high trestle near Ace Rubber.

But before the hill is a tiny neighborhood, a short walk from downtown Akron, that might otherwise be mistaken for a rural hamlet. There are two homes, old but apparently well-maintained, on the west side of Walnut and one of similar vintage and condition on the east. Another street, Aetna, intersects Walnut, and has one lovely house, painted white with green trim.

We had to drive to find a place to view Lock 11, the last of the locks we visited. We followed Wojno-Forney's car to Beech Street and a spot behind the power plant. It's an isolated triangle bordered by the plant and the Innerbelt, both rising far above, and the canal running below. It was here that our guide voiced the task force's dreams for the area—a museum in the power plant, a visitor center and gift shop at Mustill Store, and perhaps raft rides on the canal. That may seem difficult to envision, but it is no less so than the canal's construction, which took fewer than three years to build from Cleveland to Akron and only six years more to Portsmouth on the Ohio River.

NOVEMBER 1, 1992

Sharing the Secrets of the Towpath

I knew that walking the towpath of the Ohio & Erie Canal in the company of an artist would be a treat. So it made sense that trodding the trail from downtown Peninsula to the Ohio Turnpike with two artists would at least double the pleasure, especially if Joe Jesensky of Akron were one of them. Jesensky has been exploring the Cuyahoga Valley since 1918, when he was a twelve-year-old junior high school student. He still hikes with Cuyahoga Valley National Recreation Area rangers to help in their search for traces of old roads and other human intrusions on the wilderness. And he offered to guide Chuck and me along the just-restored section of the towpath from State Route 303 north along a backward S-shaped course into Boston Township. We jumped at the chance.

As we walked from Fisher's restaurant, where we met for lunch, to the towpath access road near an old railroad depot behind the Winking Lizard supper club, Jesensky reminisced about his first trips to the valley. He was a student at Willson Junior High, on the east side of Cleveland, where his family settled after its arrival from Hungary in 1911. He and other artists came armed with sketchpads and pencils, looking for scenes to draw along the banks of the river and what was left of the canal after the flood of 1913.

"You could take the train in the morning and get off at a particular spot," Jesensky said, noting that most towns between Cleveland and Akron had a depot or at least a ticket office. "It was very handy. Sometimes we would stay overnight. If it was on a Saturday, we'd stay Sunday. If it was wet weather, we'd sleep in the depot. We slept outside if it was dry."

At a place where the Cuyahoga bends sharply from north to west, about two-hundred yards north of Route 303, Jesensky stopped to point out how the terrain has changed. He unfolded a homemade map and copies of paintings and drawings of this bend in the river and the first of three canal locks we would encounter. The documents showed how the river's course was altered by a dam, which was the site of the first of several mills in Peninsula, and the location of an aqueduct that carried the canal's waters over the river just below the dam. Jesensky pointed across the river to a sandstone abutment, all that remains of the aqueduct, and said the park service plans to build a bridge to connect the west bank with the towpath.

"I noticed the last few times I've been here that the pool has been getting deeper and deeper," Jesensky said. "At one time it was quite a noticeable waterfall. Now it looks like just a rapids."

Jesensky showed us reproductions of artwork by several artists, including the late Frank Wilcox, the late Archibald Willard, and the late Daniel Webster Brown, a *Beacon Journal* editorial cartoonist. Willard came with groups of artists who made expeditions as far south as Zoar around the turn of the century, Jesensky said.

"When they got to Peninsula, they had a lot to draw," he said. "They had a heyday making sketches."

Jesensky also showed us a copy of a sketch he drew of the scene in 1928. It included a mill that burned down around 1940.

"That was a landmark," he said. "You'd come along on the train. The train would wait long enough to pick up packages and stuff and you could hear the falls and see the mill. . . . Peninsula had a lot more sketch-worthy places, a lot more than other places along the canal."

The river ran noisily in view to our left. But there were few signs in the brush that the canal had once flowed off to our right.

Jesensky shared another interesting fact about the area: "When the canal was in use, there were hardly any trees growing in here. It was all open area."

We asked him to estimate the age of the trees, but he declined, saying only that sycamores, which abound in the area, grow fast and thick at base, giving the impression they're older than they are.

Jesensky noted the towpaths were not used just for towing of canal boats. Residents used them as a way of getting from one place to another. A canal tender patrolled the towpath daily, looking for washouts and bubbles, signs of groundhogs or muskrats in the water.

This prompted Jesensky to tell the story of his friend, environmental photographer Ian Adams. Adams was out walking the towpath early one morning when he came to a clearing.

"On the other side (of the clearing) was a pair of coyotes," Jesensky said. "They stopped short and looked at him and he stopped short and looked at them. . . . Finally one of them ducked over toward the canal. The other went off on the side but didn't go very far. Finally the one that went toward the canal joined its companion. They both sat there and, believe it or not, they started to howl. They serenaded him. Ian said, 'I bet you none of the park rangers ever had that honor bestowed, and here I was without a camera.' So after that he lugged his 35 (millimeter camera) with him."

The only wildlife we saw was a toad hopping across the path and a heron flying overhead. But we saw several trees that had been visited by beavers.

MARCH 6, 1994

Snapshots in the Snow

The Ohio & Erie Canal towpath isn't as crowded with people during the winter as it is in other seasons, but the snow-covered landscape is crisscrossed with animal tracks, some of them on ice so thin you can see the water flowing beneath it.

Chuck and I decided more than a year ago that we wanted to walk the restored twenty-mile section of towpath in all four seasons. We picked a March day, when the temperature was in the twenties, for our winter excursion, and walked the section between Ira and Everett Roads.

It would be easy to dismiss the scenes along the towpath as just a lot of snow and trees. There isn't much color, but what there is all the more vivid, such as the deep green of the tall pines that line the west side of the path where we entered. The Cuyahoga River was to our right, on the east, as we headed north. Riverview Road was to our left, on the west.

The first tracks we saw were the slender imprints left by cross-country skiers. There had been other cars in the parking lot, so we weren't surprised to see a woman and man skiing toward us a short time later.

The well-packed snow trail soon gave way to a boardwalk that carried us across a beaver marsh. These wetlands were frozen over and snow-covered, so the marsh grass and thin bare tree trunks appeared to be growing out of solid ground.

A couple of strollers caught up with us when we stopped at an overlook to read a sign about the beavers and other wildlife that make the marsh their home. Chuck recalled that every bench was filled and the overlook was crowded with people when he walked this section of the path last summer. The overlook faces Riverview Road, and from it we could see the entrance to the special events site.

We had the path to ourselves until we drew near Bolanz Road. Well, almost.

There is a spot where the path practically abuts a sharp bend in the cold, gray, swift-running river. It was while we paused there that we began to feel surrounded by animals. We had seen animal tracks from the start, but at this point the river bank and areas leading to it were loaded with telltale signs of deer, rabbits, dogs, and other critters we couldn't identify.

The furry creatures themselves never came into view but their feathered counterparts were less bashful. A streak of red darted through the trees overhead. It was the first of three cardinals we saw. They appeared to be traveling together, flitting from tree to tree and standing out against the otherwise dull background. A large slate-blue and white bird, a kingfisher, literally screamed its way into and out of view. As if in competition, a small group of Canada geese honked by heading northeast in V formation. Nearby grew a thicket covered with bright red pearl-shaped berries, which, with the cardinals, were the brightest things we spotted.

Civilization came back into view as we approached Bolanz Road. The first sign was the distant view of the buildings from which the Szalay family sells sweet corn and other produce at Riverview and Bolanz during the summer.

There was a National Park Service sign, just a few yards before the path crossed Bolanz. The park provides parking across Bolanz from a small, restored farmhouse, Hunt Farm, that is sometimes open to visitors. It was closed when we were there, but we peeked through the windows from the front porch and promised ourselves we would return during the tourist season.

Just beyond Bolanz was a bridge over Furnace Run. The bridge is visible from Riverview Road, so it was a treat finally to stand on it. The view reminded us of our visit to the other more famous covered bridge over Furnace Run just a mile or so to the west. We had gone there during our walk around

Hale Farm. It had been summertime, but the vista looking west, away from the bridge, was quite similar.

And below us, in the snow that covered thin patchy ice on the water, we saw footprints of some kind of web-footed fowl. The tracks seemed too large to have been made by ducks or geese. They started at the bank and headed straight for the flowing stream.

The towpath took us by the backside of the trailer park that occupies the acreage between Riverview and the canal.

We concluded our winter walk at Lock 27, which is known as the Johnny-cake Lock. It was the fourth lock we saw. We viewed Locks 24 and 25 between Bath and Ira Roads from the car, as Riverview Road rests on the old canal bed, and stood on the rim of Lock 26 just north of Ira.

A sign told us how Lock 27 got its name, after a flood in 1828, the first experienced on the canal: "Several boats ran aground and were stranded. . . . As supplies ran low, canal passengers and crew ate only cornmeal pancakes, known as johnnycakes, and the nickname stuck for Lock 27."

As we added our own footprints to the snow between the towpath and the ranger station at Everett, we decided to start our springtime stroll at Deep Lock Quarry.

MAY 1, 1994

After the Thaw

It was nest-building time along the towpath. The fresh, clean smell of the season was in the air, the ground had thawed and the first crocuses were beginning to poke their green heads through the wet blanket of leaves on the floor of the Cuyahoga River valley. We started north from the MetroParks' Deep Lock Quarry, just south of Peninsula.

Chuck had visited the heron nests high in the trees along Bath Road between Akron-Peninsula and Riverview Roads, and reported that the big blue birds were drawing an audience of human admirers. We decided to make the herons a part of each story, regardless of where we walked along the towpath.

Two hawks soared overhead in search of a meal as we moved along a trail marked by old millstones and sandstone foundations, and from the trees came the scolding of a couple of nest-building crows.

A park sign explained that a railroad had once run along the trail, carrying millstones produced in a mill that once stood on the hill above us. All that remains today are stairs leading to the mill's foundation. The MetroParks trail led us to the towpath at Lock 28, called Deep Lock because its thirty-seven-foot lift was the highest of any lock on the canal. An old plaque on the lock's moss-covered wall bears a declaration by the Ohio Council of the American Society of Civil Engineering that the structure is a historic example of civil engineering.

We could hear the Cuyahoga River before the towpath brought us to its west bank and the first of several rapids we would see. The bank had been reinforced with rocks and other material held together by metal cagelike structures. On the opposite shore we could see the backside of the Brandywine Golf Course.

Another sign informed us that a trail off the towpath led to what had been the Cleveland Stone Company's Quarry No. 15, a portion of which was purchased in 1879 by Ferdinand Schumacher to make millstones for his Akron business, the American Cereal Works, predecessor to the Quaker Oats Company.

A new bridge—built in 1992 of steel with a wooden deck—carried the towpath over a swift-moving tributary of the Cuyahoga a short distance from the bridge that carries state Route 303 over the river at Peninsula. From the towpath, we saw Peninsula as no motorist has ever seen it. From our low vantage point south of the bridge, we could see the shadows of people walking across the bridge but not the people themselves.

North of Route 303 we came to another old foundation. A sign and photograph told us that the Moody & Thomas Mill had stood there, near the footbridge that carries the towpath over the river.

We had walked a section of the trail north of that point before the tow-

The towpath trail runs through a tunnel near Deep Lock Quarry.

path was open to the public, so the next two miles were familiar, but not without some pleasant surprises. One was at Lock 31, where we learned from another park sign that the name Lonesome Lock was derived from the virtual isolation of its location from the river.

Dark storm clouds began to gather in the northwestern sky as we approached Stumpy Basin, so named because it was wide enough to allow canalboats to turn around, stop over, and be stored for the winter. A boardwalk carries the towpath over the marsh that led to the basin, which was marked by a sign and old photos of ice cutters and ice skaters. Two Canada geese honked overhead, drawing our eyes just as they glided in for a landing on the river. They swam to the opposite bank, where the rest of the flock covered a wide, sandy section.

The Ohio Turnpike runs just north of Stumpy Basin, and the towpath meanders along a section of water-filled canal. It started to rain as we approached the eastbound lane of I-271, so we opened our umbrellas and pressed on. It was just a brief shower, and the birds were singing when we walked into the hamlet of Boston, where the towpath crosses Boston Mills Road just east of Riverview Road.

Adjacent to the towpath, boarded up and with signs posted warning trespassers that it is owned by the United States Government, is the general store built by the Boston Land and Manufacturing Company in 1836, thirty years after surveyor James Stanford settled there. (It is now a National Park canal museum.)

The towpath was lonely after we walked north of the Boston Mills ski slopes. Our presence frightened a flock of ducks, which took to the air from a marshy pond near Lock 33. Our feet told us it was time to stop walking before we arrived at the vacant buildings that once housed the Jaite Paper Mill on West Highland Road in Sagamore Hills. There, the towpath crosses the road and continues north from Lock 34, known as Red Lock, but we decided to save that for our summer visit.

AUGUST 7, 1994

Summer on the Towpath

A lone deer sauntered across Highland Road in Sagamore Hills Township as I approached the parking lot at Red Lock, which was to be the southern terminus of our summer walk on the towpath. Chuck and I chose the first day of summer to explore the towpath between Red Lock and State Route 82 three miles to the north. We arrived in separate cars, left mine in the parking lot, and drove north in his to the Cleveland MetroParks' Brecksville Reservation, where we parked off Riverview Road in a lot serving the 113-year-old Station Road Bridge.

If you have never seen the wrought-iron truss bridge, it is worth a special trip. Station Road Bridge was built by the Massillon Bridge Company in 1881 and wears signs at each end to prove it. It was the major carrier of traffic—first horse-drawn, then motorized—across the river between Brecksville and Sagamore Hills until the high-level Route 82 span was built just to the north in 1931. The Station Road Bridge continued to carry vehicles until it was closed in 1979.

By then it was badly rusted and might have simply been removed had it not been in the Cuyahoga Valley National Recreation Area. John Debo, the park's superintendent, promised it would be rebuilt, and it was, although it took several years for the $385,755 needed to be allocated. The bridge was dismantled in February of 1992 and hauled off to be made new by Deck Incorporated in Elmira, New York. It was rededicated eight months later and today carries hikers, bikers, and horseback riders to paths on both sides of the river.

Our destination was the towpath, which hugged the opposite bank. We paused to admire the way the world was reflected in the river. It had stormed the night before, and the morning mist still clung to many trees.

It was a short distance to the towpath, past some large shale outcroppings and trees that bore telltale signs of recent visits by a beaver or two. Station Road, or what's left of it, begins its steep upward climb just east of the towpath, and we tried to visualize what the traffic pattern at this crossroads might have been during the canal's heyday.

Before beginning our trek south, we detoured north to examine the Route 82 bridge up close. Across the river, a man in a blue cap sat fishing on the sandy west bank halfway between the two bridges. The concrete arches of the Route 82 bridge towered majestically overhead, and when we looked to the east, we discovered that, if we stood in the right spot, all we could see of the sun was a shaft of light cutting through the last of the mist.

We started south, hoping to cover the two and a half miles to Red Lock before the comfortable day turned into the predicted scorcher. On our left, east of the towpath, the canal looked positively primordial. It was littered with tree limbs and, from the sound of it, inhabited by a regiment of frogs.

Chuck froze in his tracks and whispered: "There's a beaver."

He was right, and for once I saw more than a circle in the water where one had been. A dozen yards away, amid a cluster of floating branches, the animal struggled to be invisible while we, too, tried to blend in with the scenery. We were prepared to outwait the critter, but the conversation of two approaching women scared the beaver away. It was gone before they got close enough to realize what they had missed.

The canal dried up a short distance beyond the beaver sighting, so we turned our attention to the river, where we spotted a heron standing in the shallows near a sandbar. A few feet away, a lone goose stood on the sand, honking as if to warn the fish that the long-legged predator was there. A fish jumped, leaving an ever-widening circle on the water, and, as if in response, the heron struck, its head darting below the surface.

A tall tree, recently felled by a human, formed a natural bridge across the canal, and hanging from it was debris from this spring, when the water was higher. We had to sidestep a large branch from another tree, which had apparently fallen across the path during the previous night's storm.

It started to rain—or so we thought—until we realized the wind was blowing the heavy downpour from the trees above. It started and stopped as the breeze ebbed and flowed.

Strollers cross the Station Road Bridge in Brecksville.

I learned the difference between dragonflies and damselflies as we continued walking south. The wings of dragonflies are spread open when they're at rest, while the damselflies fold theirs. We saw both in abundance, as well as the tiniest toad—no bigger than my thumbnail—and a beetle, metallic green in color. We saw no deer but found the tracks of one in a muddy clearing off the towpath. The flora along the way included swamp roses, which bloomed as if planted on the edge of the path; duckweed on the surface of the canal water; and a field of daisies underlaid with a carpet of clover.

At the south end of the Old Carriage Trail, which loops away from the towpath and back again, we came to Goose Pond Weir, one of several weirs, or dams, built to control the canal's water level. Anything in excess of four feet was diverted to the river, a sign informed us.

Red Lock was a welcome sight. The promised heat and high humidity were upon us, and our thoughts turned to iced tea and air conditioning. We never did learn how the lock got its name. A park sign said it might have been because of red clay found in the area, or because of the red paint used on its gate.

A fisherman in a blue hat—probably the one we saw at the start of our walk—was packing his gear when Chuck dropped me off at the parking lot. I asked about his catch.

"Just a few bluegills," he said. "They're jumping but not biting. They have more sense than humans. They don't eat in hot weather."

OCTOBER 2, 1994

A Change of Color

The herons' nests on Bath Road were empty. It was a fitting conclusion to our four-part exploration of nearly twenty miles of towpath between Akron and the Cuyahoga County community of Valley View. We had started at the south end when the herons were nesting at the tops of bare trees in the marsh between Akron-Peninsula and Riverview roads . . . and by summer the sleek birds had become a symbol of our series. Now, as the first colors of autumn were making their appearance, the only sign of the herons was a lone bird, airborne near the nesting site.

But that's the end of the story.

It began at Wilson's Mill on Canal Road at Fitzwater Road, just south of Alexander Road in Valley View. Fitzwater crosses the canal and the Cuyahoga River, only to dead-end a short distance to the west. A generation ago, if memory serves me correctly, it continued west to Riverview Road. Flooding caused community decision-makers to erect a permanent barricade.

Wilson's Mill is at Lock 37. The foundation is a blend of ivy-covered old sandstone and, where repairs have been made, cinderblock. A water wheel at the north end of the building, powered by the spillway from Lock 37, used to grind wheat into flour. We walked perhaps two hundred feet to the first bridge, crossed over the canal to the towpath, and started south. A park sign at the lock informed us it was three miles to the Station Road Bridge. The sign also contained hand-colored old photos under glass. One showed a group of people admiring an early motorcar on the towpath between the canal and the river. Another showed a woman peeking out the door of a house near the lock as a canal boat either arrived or departed.

The back view of Wilson's Mill revealed it to be larger than it appears from the road. A flock of pigeons occupied the roof of one of several buildings that line the canal's east bank behind the mill. Nearby grew a cluster of sunflowers, which helped explain the birds' presence.

Originally called Alexander's Mill, it was built in 1855 and probably used a wooden water wheel in its early days. According to the wayside sign, "The mill was refitted with turbines during the late 1800s. The top of a turbine can still be seen in the spillway channel. After 1900, the mill made a successful transition from flour to feed milling, reflecting changes occurring nationwide. It continued to use waterpower until 1970. Alexander's Mill was the last to use water power and is the only remaining mill in Cuyahoga County."

The sign contained two more colorized old photos under glass. One, undated, shows the Vanochek family tavern, general store, house, and barn at

Lock 37. In the second, the mill provided the background for a shot of a Sunday family excursion on the canal in 1890. The Wilson family has operated the mill since 1899.

Chuck spotted deer tracks in the mud on the west bank as we continued walking south. Upon closer examination, we saw muddy imprints of a variety of smaller animals, but, as we would find in the next couple of hours, the animals themselves were nowhere to be seen.

Looking east, we had a clear view across Canal Road and up a steep grassy hillside to a fence and a line of trees at the top. We could see cattle grazing on the hillside from a vantage point a dozen steps down the path.

We came to the red brick Frazee-Hynton House, which predates the canal. Built as a stagecoach stop in 1806, it was a private residence for many years, and is now owned by the National Park Service. We crossed the canal and the road for a closer look and could see signs of repairs made in preparation for a planned restoration in 1992.

At Sagamore Road, we crossed into Summit County. There, Canal Road becomes Valleyview Road and continues south and then east, away from the towpath. The towpath began a series of sharp bends because of the hilly terrain. The runoff from the hills has created a series of deltas, making this section of the canal look more like a river than a manmade channel.

The tracks that carry the Cuyahoga Valley Scenic Railroad between Akron and Cleveland came into view as we approached a near-U-turn bend in the canal, but we didn't see any rail traffic until we crossed under the bridge carrying Route 82 over the valley. An engine, equipped with a small crane, pulled a single car, a maintenance vehicle, and crew.

As we neared the end of our walk, the pedestrian and bicycle traffic increased and included a man pushing himself along the trail in a wheelchair. His pace, like ours, was more leisurely than the pace of the joggers, whose expressions suggested they weren't enjoying the sights as much as we did.

Canal Road traffic passes Wilson's Mill in Valley View.

MAY 14, 2000

Home to Roost

How's this for a different kind of Mother's Day story? Instead on focusing on just one mother, we decided to take a walk in one of the most popular nature spots in the Cuyahoga River Valley to watch 148 mothers—and a like number of fathers—at work.

Chuck was already at work sketching when I parked my car on the northern berm of West Bath Road. It was a little after nine on a weekday morning, but other cars were parked there and several more had already come and gone during the forty-five minutes he had been there. The attraction was the herons' roost in the swamp just south of Bath, between Akron-Peninsula and Riverview roads. The roost's popularity is no surprise. One visit, and the image of these graceful, long-legged birds in flight above their treetop nests is certain to be etched in your mind forever. But you'll probably keep driving down that short stretch of road to see it all again and again, as we have done for nearly ten years, just in case something changes.

By midsummer, a descriptive panel informing the readers of everything they may ever want to know about the lifestyles of blue herons will be in place, courtesy of the Cuyahoga Valley Association and a grant from Leadership Akron. Peg Bobel and Andrea Irland (then, respectively, Cuyahoga Valley Association associate director and administrative assistant) visit the roost every week to explain to tourists just what it is they're looking at. Armed with clipboards, they count the herons, not people.

"The main reason we're there is to monitor the birds," Bobel said. "Educating people is a byproduct."

Last year was a record year for the heron population at this roost—123 nests and 350 chicks—and this year there are 148 nests. Which brings up the question of how one counts herons.

It begins with the nests, Bobel said. "That number has increased every year since we have started monitoring the site," she said. "One tree had fifty nests."

Ducks, geese, and a buzzard were seen in addition to the roosting herons.

Irland said she and Bobel know eggs have hatched when the adults stand at attention in the nests. Counting the chicks is more difficult because they're so small. For this a "really good" pair of binoculars and a device called a spotting scope are needed, Bobel said. "This is looking like a good year," Irland said. "Some herons were just building nests when the first eggs were hatching in others." The hatching watch will continue until the foliage gets too thick.

Our hatch watch was limited to part of one morning, but we learned a great deal, thanks to Bobel and Irland (both of whom have left the association). For instance, herons were nearly extinct a hundred years ago because so many were shot to provide feathers for women's hats. They were also killed because they fished at trout hatcheries. Eventually better—and more humane—ways were found to shoo them away. The resurgence of herons has been linked to the return of beavers, which build the wetlands where the big birds thrive, Bobel said.

The Bath Road roost, on Akron-owned land adjacent to the city's sewage treatment plant, is one of three in or just outside of the Cuyahoga Valley National Recreation Area. The second, north of State Route 82 in Brecksville, is visible from the Ohio & Erie Canal Towpath and has been known for some time. The third was discovered just last year in Furnace Run MetroPark. All three are being monitored. There also are active heron roosts in Kent, the Portage Lakes area, Twinsburg Township, and Solon.

AKRON CITY MAGAZINE,
SEPTEMBER–DECEMBER 2003

Towpath Is a "Staircase" of Discovery

A woman walking her dog approached the north end of Lock 15 as Chuck sized up the Ohio & Erie Canal Towpath scene for his illustration one evening this summer. It was so different from our first visit in 1990, when all that greeted us north of the lock was a wall of green, where the forest had reclaimed the towpath in the years since the great flood of 1913.

A woman walks her dog along the towpath trail at Mustill's Store in 2003.

Our guide thirteen years ago was Cascade Locks Park Association founder Virginia Wojno-Forney, who spelled out the group's dreams for the Mustill Store and the milelong "staircase" locks area, so called because of the grade, steepest of the 309-mile canal.

The association's members-appreciation night prompted Chuck's 2003 visit to Lock 15 and the restored Mustill Store. I couldn't be there, so I walked the trail later, knowing that Chuck is as good a reporter as he is an artist.

Executive director Bridget Garvin's discussion of the association's projects and upcoming plans were a highlight of the evening, Chuck said. I visited Garvin's office on the second floor of the Mustill Store to learn about the projects before I headed north on the trail between Lock 15 and Memorial Parkway.

The first project is the search for the steel millwheel believed to be buried on the site of Ferdinand Schumacher's Cascade Mills on the south side of North Street. The association, working with the University of Akron Department of Classical Studies, Anthropology and Archaeology on the dig this fall, hopes to develop the mill site as an interactive, educational visitor destination.

Another plan involves preserving, interpreting, and celebrating the African American history, cultural legacy, and jazz that once was centered on Howard Street, within what is now the Cascade Locks Park. A committee formed in December of 2002 to explore this project.

The association also is developing electronic archives at the Mustill Store. A grant from the Ohio Humanities Council is providing start-up costs. The archives, when operational, will be available to the public. (The association's website in 2004 was www.cascadelocks.org.)

CHAPTER EIGHT

Walking the Bases

*Akron's love affair with baseball goes back almost to the time when the name of the game
was "base ball"—two words. My interest in that history—if not the game itself—and
Chuck's personal fondness for Civil War-era base ball resulted in more than one enjoy-
able afternoon along the first and third baselines. The article published September 3,
1995, also titled "Walking the Bases," seems like an appropriate place to begin.*

A young man tooting a tin whistle sat on a hay bale as players for the
Canal Fulton Mules and the Chagrin Falls Forest Citys warmed up on a flat,
bumpy field next to the blacksmith shop at Hale Farm and Village. Nearby,
several women in ankle-length hoop skirts and wide-brimmed hats visited in
the shade of a tree, and a white-maned, mustachioed Mark Twain look-
alike—dressed in white shirt, bow tie, black vest, and gray dress pants—
sprawled on a picnic blanket, his top hat and walking stick at his side.

Except for an occasional passing car, it might have been a scene from the
summer of 1865 instead of 1995, and no wonder. The teams were there to
play Civil War–era base ball, a game that displayed manners of the kind
George Bush must have had in mind when (as president) he spoke of a
kinder, gentler nation. Adding to the atmosphere, the guitar-and-banjo duo
Sassafras strummed vintage melodies from a shady spot on the sidelines, and

Scott Burr, the twelve-year-old bat boy, chewed on a long piece of straw, looking like central casting's candidate for Tom Sawyer.

It was my first old-time base ball game, but Chuck had been encouraging me to attend one since he discovered the sport a year earlier and saw it as another chance to take a walk through history. Two weeks earlier, the Summit County Historical Society Merinos played the Ohio Village Muffins at Hardesty Park in Akron (a scene he captured in his sketchpad). The Muffins of Columbus inspired the revival of the old-time game in 1981 and hold the distinction of having played a game at Jacobs Field in Cleveland before the Indians. The Merinos' captain, Steve Paschen (then director of the Summit Historical Society), told Chuck he hopes to arrange a similar first for the Summit team when Akron's minor league ballpark is built. The team, organized three years ago, is named for the Merino sheep that once grazed on the lawn at the Perkins Stone Mansion in Akron.

Chuck and I met at Hale Farm as the Mules and Forest Citys were warming up two Sundays later. Hay bales along the first and third baselines separated the spectators, called cranks, from the playing field.

At 2 P.M., the Mark Twain look-alike brushed himself off, put on his top hat, and strode onto the field. He was, I learned, Serapio "Scrap" Zalba, president of the Chagrin Falls Historical Society and the umpire. Zalba instructed the teams to line up on the field and introduced team captains Ed Shuman of the Mules and Bo Burr (Scott's father) of the Forest Citys, who, in turn, introduced their players to the cranks. Then, after the stone toss, which was won by the Mules, the umpire yelled, "Striker to the line !"

This is where a bit of crank education might come in handy. The ball is presented to the striker by the hurler. The striker's job is to hit the ball and, with any luck, make it around the bases to score an ace. The player must go to the scorers' table and say, "Tally me, please, sir," then ring a bell. If the scorer is a woman, the proper request would be "Tally me, please, ma'am."

The first striker got a double and arrived at second base to a chorus of "Well struck, sir" from teammates and cranks. Bases were loaded when the

The Summit County Historical Society Merinos and the Ohio Village Muffins play vintage base ball at Hardesty Park in Akron.

fourth striker straddled the line at home plate and pounded the ball into the centerfielder's hands. "The striker is dead!" proclaimed the umpire.

During the next seven innings, I learned that a striker is dead if the ball is caught on a fly or first bounce, only team captains may speak to the umpire, and those guilty of breaches of manners, such as cursing, spitting, or allowing one's shirt tail to come untucked, are subject to fines. When a bat slipped out of a striker's hand, the umpire shouted, "An ungentlemanly act, sir! That will be a fine of one day's wages—twenty-five cents." The honor system and good sportsmanship were at work, so on a close play at home plate, the umpire asked the runner if he was tagged out before declaring it a double play, and both sides yelled "Huzzah!" when the rightfielder made a spectacular over-the-shoulder catch.

Activity on the sidelines was as interesting as what was happening on the field. Burr and Shuman fanned themselves with stacks of play money in attempts to bribe the umpire, who occasionally took a nip from a flask.

"We have three objectives—to interpret history, put on a good show, and play serious baseball," Burr told us. "We will at times sacrifice serious baseball to demonstrate a point of history."

When he wasn't in the field, Forest Citys player Ron Ciocca Jr. of Macedonia pitched a plastic ball to his three-year-old son, Anthony, who gave new meaning to the Batman logo on his tank top. The child rarely missed with his plastic bat, and when he did, he demonstrated a good arm and eye throwing the ball back to his father. His grandfather, Ron Ciocca Sr. of Bainbridge, in Geauga County, also plays for the Forest Citys. Anthony got to play, too, when the game was reconfigured from what Bo Burr described as 1858 New York rules to 1858 Massachusetts rules. At the end of the seventh inning, umpire Zalba called for the cranks to join the players on the field. By mutual agreement, the game was over, with the Forest Citys winning 21 to 6, so everyone could have a chance to take part in the action.

"This is an experiment we haven't done before," Burr told the crowd. "You can help us learn the Massachusetts game ourselves. We've never played it before, except for my family, at Cooperstown, where we learned it two weeks ago."

That's Cooperstown, New York, home of the Baseball Hall of Fame and Museum.

The bases were taken up and in their places three-foot stakes were pounded into the ground. Any contact between the bat and the ball, which was smaller and softer than the New York ball, constituted a hit, Burr said, so what the New York rules called a "foul tick" was playable with the Massachusetts rules. Each inning would have one out, achieved by catching a ball on the fly or by plugging the runner—hitting the runner with the ball before he reached a stake.

After the regulars played a demonstration inning, the cranks were invited to play on the team of their choice. There was no limit to the number of players on a team.

Anthony swung and "ticked" the ball, then began to cry because he didn't understand that that was as good as a long fly to centerfield.

SEPTEMBER 7, 1997

Ghosts on a Faded Field

A man resembling a Roman chariot driver stood astride the back end of a plow-sized lawn mower that was feasting on the big grassy field at Carroll and Beaver Streets. He and his companion, who walked behind a second mower, looked like the grounds crew at a baseball park, which the field was, once upon a time.

The inspiration for our visit to this Akron residential neighborhood, which has coexisted with commerce and industry for many years, was a photo in Richard McBane's book *Glory Days: The Akron Yankees of the Middle Atlantic League,* published earlier this year by the Summit County Historical Society Press. The photo shows the same field on May 5, 1920, during the Akron Numatics' home opener against a team from Jersey City, New Jersey. The Numatics played in the International League for just that one year, and by 1923, League Park had been razed and the field was being used as a farmers' market. (It would be another five years before professional baseball would return to Akron at a new League Park on Crosier Street near Summit Lake. That stadium is also long gone.)

A chain-link fence topped with three rows of barbed wire separates the old League Park site from the rest of the neighborhood. Gnarled remnants of branches—from hedges that once grew along and through the fence—remain securely lodged in the metal links, where they were left because they were too thick to remove when the hedges were cut down.

A faded sign on the Carroll Street side of the fence is illegible from a distance, but up close we could make out the words: "The Summit Growers Market C" and "Tuesday, Thursday and Saturday Mornings." The market operated there fifty-three years, according to McBane. Today the well-manicured site is home to Waste Management of Ohio.

The old League Park site intrigued us because, as McBane wrote in the photo caption, Olympic star Jim Thorpe, a member of the Numatics, was in the on-deck circle when Harry E. Williams shot the picture. Another reason is that the 1920 photo depicted an Akron neighborhood in the final year of a population boom that doubled the city's size.

Chuck and I went searching for signs of the old park, wondering if we could even recognize the site today. We not only recognized it but were able to approximate where the photographer stood when he snapped his picture, because the field has remained a field all these years.

Trees south of the field today block most of the homes that were visible along the horizon seventy-seven years ago, but those that can be seen from Carroll and Beaver are recognizable in the photo. From our contemporary vantage point, ten paces east of Beaver on the north side of Carroll, we guessed the houses beyond the tree line were south of Exchange Street, in the vicinity of Mason Park. We guessed wrong. They line the north side of Excelsior Avenue, a short street that runs between Beaver and Cleveland Streets.

We learned that by heading south along Beaver toward Exchange, crossing a long-idled section of B & O Railroad tracks, and passing the British Petroleum's Akron Bulk Plant and Retail Training Center. Excelsior forms the southern boundary of BP's property. It is still a thriving residential street. Children, on summer vacation, played on the sidewalk. They paid us no heed. Neither did the adults who sat on the front porches of several houses. We walked east along Excelsior to Windsor Street, which dead-ends at a bluff

League Park, home field of the Akron Numatics in 1920, is seen in contrast with a contemporary view of the Carroll Street site. Jim Thorpe played for the Numatics.

cleaned and trimmed, as if for a military inspection. Even the trash cans appeared to have been placed at just the right intervals.

It was my first visit to the recreation facility that was built by Firestone in 1925 and turned over to the city of Akron in March of 1988. Chuck, who watched his father play softball there when he was a child, was returning for the second time this year. Across the street, at the northeast corner, is the building housing the Great Trail Council of the Boy Scouts of America. At the southeast corner is a blocklong stretch of lawn leading to the Harvey S. Firestone Memorial.

There are two diamonds at the field, one in front of the stadium and another, at the southwest corner of the block, in front of a small set of bleachers. So it is possible to hit a home run from one diamond to the other. There were no home runs or even foul balls hit while we were there. It was shortly before noon, and not a soul was in sight.

We walked around the block to the stadium entrance, past two brightly painted but empty ticket booths and through the open gate, in search of someone who could tell us about the place. We found Howard Johnson, the Akron Recreation Bureau's coordinator of athletic fields, and Dennis Harrill, one of the two men who keep the place looking so neat. They gave us a tour, from the rafters, where two lifelike owl statues fail to fool the birds they were intended to scare away, to the former Firestone pistol range in a lower-level addition on the east end.

Until recently, the range was used by the Akron Police Department. Shortly after the city took possession of the stadium, Bernie Factor, president of the Akron Amateur Softball Commission, began lobbying to make it the home of the Summit County Softball Hall of Fame, which inducted its first twenty-four members in 1986. Volunteers had completed installation of heating ducts and wall studs and were preparing to start the paneling when we visited. The Hall of Fame will be ready in time for this year's induction of twelve new members.

There is something restful about sitting in the stands when there's no one else around. It wasn't just our thought, we discovered. People are always asking Johnson's permissions to sit there for peaceful picnic lunches when no games are being played. Outside, the noontime walkers were beginning to appear. You know the ones—officebound women and men who trade their dress shoes for walking shoes for an hour's exercise each day.

We decided to join them, but at a pace more conducive to image- and impression-gathering. At Wilbeth and Firestone Parkway, Chuck stopped to draw while I explored the residential-commercial stretch on the south side of Wilbeth. The homes are older there than across Main in Firestone Park, but for the most part are well maintained. I stopped at Wilbeth and Hackberry Street, remembering when the corner tavern, now called the Exchequer, was a restaurant operated by hypnotist Ted Boyer. From a distance, the property next door appeared to be vacant. But walking by on the sidewalk, I could see a house shielded by trees and a wide side yard occupied by a least three dog-houses.

At 64 Wilbeth, the parking lot was beginning to fill up for St. Macedono-Bulgarian Orthodox Church's luncheon, which is served form 11 A.M. to 2 P.M. every Tuesday. The schedule didn't allow us to stop to sample the wonderful ethnic food *Beacon Journal* colleague Fran Murphey (now deceased) had introduced me to.

Back on Main Street, we paused to look at where we had been. The slope of the sidewalk is just right for skateboards. Looking southwest from that higher elevation, we could see the Akron Baptist Temple on Manchester Road on the horizon. Studying Downtown Automatic Transmission and Broadway Motors at the southwest corner of Main and Wilbeth, we wondered just where "downtown" ends.

Saving the best for last, we crossed Main and walked the path to the Firestone Memorial. It should be a "must stop" on any tour of Akron. At the center of a five-tiered circle of stone is a larger-than-life statue of Harvey S. Firestone, robed and seated in a contemplative attitude. It is impressive from a distance, which is the way most passersby see it. But from a distance they miss the details, such as the signature of artist James Earle Fraser on the west side of the base. And they miss the frieze on the semicircular wall behind the statue. From across the expanse of lawn, the wall appears to have some sort of design. But up close, the design is seen to be words of praise for Firestone, set against an art-deco background of reclining figures, clouds, sunbursts, and rosettes.

Vandals have removed the noses from the figures, but the memorial is otherwise intact. Reading the inscriptions, I learned that Firestone was born on December 20, 1868, and died the day I was born, February 7, 1938. And I was reminded of some things worth mentioning again: "He transformed a gift of nature to the benefit of all mankind. . . . The inspiration of his life is an enduring heritage. . . . Devoted to church and home, he brought out the best in others and gave the best of himself."

APRIL 11, 1999

Catching a Baseball Memory or Two

We went searching for some old baseball memories, but all we found on the grassy field at Crosier and Victory streets were a couple of soccer goals. The field—adjacent to and used by Saturn School, the Akron Public Schools' program designed to help students expelled for nonviolent offenses keep up with schoolwork—bears no signs that it once was the site of League Park, where the Akron Yankees played from 1935 through 1941.

The view from the entrance to the school's parking lot at Paris Avenue and Victory was somewhat disappointing, but it improved as we walked north along the chain-link fence that forms the field's eastern boundary. Chuck found nothing to illustrate there, but we discovered that when we looked northwest across the old League Park site, we had a clear, if distant, view of the baseball diamonds at Akron's Summit Lake Park. The diamonds are on the east bank of the ninety-three-acre lake, just north of where Summit Beach Park operated from the early 1900s until 1959.

So we hightailed it down Crosier and across Lakeshore Boulevard and were greeted by a sign identifying the ballpark as George Sisler Field. How's that for a memory-evoking name? Richard McBane began his book *Glory Days: The Akron Yankees of the Middle Atlantic League, 1935–1941* with an account of Sisler's last playing appearance before hometown fans in an exhibition game in 1928. And *Beacon Journal* columnist Bob Dyer is still lamenting the fact that Akron officials didn't name Canal Park stadium for Sisler, a native of the Manchester area who was inducted into the Baseball Hall of Fame at Cooperstown in 1939.

Sisler never played for the Yankees—Akron's or New York's. He spent most of his fifteen-year career with the St. Louis Browns, and was playing for the Boston Braves in 1928. The game McBane wrote about in his opening chapter, titled "Before the Yankees," was an exhibition against Akron's General Tire team. Sisler, described by baseball legend Ty Cobb as "the nearest thing to a perfect ballplayer," was a left-hander who might have become a major-league pitching great if he hadn't hit and fielded so well, according to every account I've read about him. He died on March 26, 1973, in St. Louis, two days after his eightieth birthday.

McBane's baseball book inspired us to find the League Park site, just as it had two years earlier when we visited the site of Akron's original League Park at Carroll and Beaver streets. The "new" League Park was built in 1928 for $135,000, and was home to the Akron Tyrites of the Central League. The team and the league became victims of the Depression. Both were gone by 1932. In his book, McBane wrote that the Akron Black Tyrites of the Negro National League played in League Park in 1933, and that after the Yankees' farm team left Akron in 1941, the field was home to amateur baseball and football.

We walked a diagonal path across one of two baseball diamonds at Sisler Field, stopping from time to time to look back, hoping to find a perspective that would showcase both the League Park site and the contemporary playing fields. We found the right vantage point when we got to West South Street, a few paces east of where the Ohio & Erie Canal enters Summit Lake. From there, green fences curve gently around the playing fields, and the stadium lights and the red-topped right field foul pole frame the League Park site in the distance. To complete the illustration and capture the baseball memory we sought, Chuck decided to include a sketch of Sisler.

Looking south from the bridge over the canal, we watched a crow seeking lunch from a treetop and remembered our encounter with a noisy and nosy swan when we walked along the lake's western shore in January 1990. That visit had sent me scrambling for a reference book to identify the chicken-sized, web-footed black birds with pointy white beaks that came begging for food along with gulls, mallards, and Canada geese. They were American coots, and, we're happy to report, they were well represented this spring, as were the gulls, mallards, and geese. But they weren't begging this time, as we followed the bike path along the east bank to the Summit Lake Community Center and the Sisler Field sign.

APRIL 3, 1994

Batter Up

The giant metal light poles that ring Thurman Munson Memorial Stadium were swaying as much as three feet in the wind. We had not yet seen the season's last snowfall, and protective tarps covered the pitcher's mound and the areas around home plate and the bases. It was hardly a day for baseball, but that didn't matter to a couple of overgrown kids who dropped by for a pre-season look at the ballpark on Canton's south side.

With all the hoopla surrounding Jacobs Field, the Cleveland Indians' new stadium in the Gateway sports complex in Cleveland, it would be easy for its local farm team to get lost in the shuffle, so we decided to take a walk around the home of the Canton-Akron Indians of the AA Eastern League. General Manager Jeff Auman welcomed us and turned us over to Brent Horvath, the team's public relations director, for a brief orientation. Then we had the park to ourselves. The stadium is at 2501 Allen Avenue S.E., just off Canton's Cleveland Avenue, about two minutes from Interstate 77 Exit 103.

The Akron-born Thurman Lee Munson lived on Cleveland Avenue from age eight, in 1955, until he entered Kent State University. The 1965 Canton Lehman High School graduate had starred in basketball, football, and baseball by the time the New York Yankees signed him as their catcher in 1968. He was at the top of his career when he was killed in August 1979 while practicing landings in his private plane at the Akron-Canton Airport. In life, Thurman Munson was often described as a "natural"—high praise for an athlete. Veteran *Beacon Journal* sports writer Milan Zban, who played minor league baseball, says that the park that bears Munson's name is one of the finest he has seen.

The aluminum stands were empty, but our footfalls on the stairs were a reminder of the tattoo of ten thousand feet as fans rally their support for the home team. Chuck recalled hearing that thunderous sound before he entered the stadium on his first visit a few seasons ago.

Munson Stadium has seating for seven thousand in twenty rows behind home plate and along the first and third base lines. Often five thousand of the seats are filled, Horvath said. "We have good crowds, especially after the kids get out of school," he said. Last year's attendance was 273,000—an average of thirty-nine hundred for the seventy-game season. The league's worst team last season, the Reading Phillies, had the best draw, 313,000, Horvath said. Rain appears to be the only thing that keeps people away.

People enjoy AA baseball because the players are almost ready for the majors or, in some cases, have just come from the majors to work out problems.

"It's a good brand of baseball, and it doesn't cost $25," Horvath said.

Boy and Girl Scouts have their night at Munson Stadium. They get to parade around the field in their uniforms. We walked the parade route—the fine gravel track that circles the playing field—and took a close-up look at the billboards that line the outfield fence. It was my first visit to the park, but the views were reminiscent of almost every baseball-themed movie I have ever seen—from *Pride of the Yankees* to *Bull Durham.*

A bank billboard invites every batter to hit the ball through the second zero of the figure $15,000. The target is cut out and twice the size of the other zeros.

The stands and bleachers were empty when we visited Thurman Munson
Memorial Stadium in Canton.

A church bought billboard space next to that of a beer company. The message—"Let's party forever"—is illustrated by the crosses of Calvary silhouetted against a balloon-filled sky. You could almost see some future Babe Ruth with the bat on his shoulder and pointing his index finger at the Calvary scene, the hollow zero, or, more likely, the four-hundred-foot marker in the center of the field.

We paused beneath the marker and commented on how much shorter the distance appears to be from that perspective than it does from home plate.

The bullpen, near the left field foul line, had room for two pitchers and catchers. It reminded me of my favorite place to sit at Cleveland Municipal Stadium when I was a preteen attending games on my own for the first time in the 1950s. The pitchers always made time for the kids in the stands before game time. "The Bear," Mike Garcia, was my favorite, even though he sometimes had to remind us we were there to watch the game and not make conversation.

My story reminded Chuck of the day he met Woody Held and Vic Power as a prize for winning a *Beacon Journal* Kids' Page drawing contest. He wanted to meet superstar Rocky Colavito, but the Rock was busy at batting practice. Chuck followed Held's and Power's careers for years after that meeting.

Fans get to know the Canton-Akron Indians players, too. "Kids see them at baseball camps we put on," Horvath said. And they remember the players when they move on to the majors. The club inaugurated two programs to bring young fans to the ballpark last year. Every student in Stark, Summit, and Tuscarawas Counties was able to get one free ticket through the schools. Also, all high school varsity baseball players in the three counties got a free pass, good for ten games.

We stopped at the home-team dugout on our way back to home plate. The red background and team logo had been freshly painted. In fact, the paint can and brush were still where the painter had left them. There seemed to be only one thing left to say: *Play ball!*

FEBRUARY 2, 1997

Walking the Bases—Again

Our snow trek mission was to boldly go where no fan has gone before. With opening day three months away, we wanted to walk the bases at Canal Park, Akron's new Class AA baseball stadium, to get the player's-eye view of the place. Lou Ciraldo, project manager for Summit Construction, promised to show us around, but Chuck and I were worried that the winter's on-again, off-again rainy weather would prevent us from getting onto the field. We needn't have worried. Ciraldo picked a day when the wind chill guaranteed our feet would do no damage to the snow-covered grass.

In a way, this was like the final chapter of a trilogy that began when we visited Thurman Munson Memorial Stadium in Canton before the 1994 season. We didn't know it then, but talks about moving the minor-league team to Akron were already taking place. After the move was a done deal, we walked around the Canal Park site in downtown Akron for a story that was published in August 1995.

Akron Service Director Joe Kidder also was our guide for the indoor portion of our recent tour of Canal Park. We started in the nearly completed 144-seat sports bar and restaurant at the State Street end of the stadium, then continued on to the souvenir store, the loges on the upper level, and, beneath the stands, to the home team and visitor locker rooms, training and exercise areas, and indoor batting practice area, complete with two pitching mounds. A worker was installing spike-proof flooring in both dugouts, which were still covered with plastic sheeting to keep out the weather until the benches, made in downtown Akron by the Plastic Lumber Company, could be installed. On our way outside, our guides showed us two chairlifts that make it possible for disabled people to get to the playing field.

"I feel like a kid," Ciraldo said when we trudged out to the tarp-covered pitcher's mound. I seconded that emotion as Chuck clicked away with his camera, adding to his scrapbook of construction photos that date to when the

We took a winter preview look at the new Canal Park.

Anthony Wayne Hotel was imploded—and imploded—and imploded—to make way for the stadium. That was January 21, 1996, and here we were, just a year later, shaking off signs from an imaginary catcher behind home plate. Even more remarkable was the fact that it was only two years—almost to the day, January 17, 1995—since Akron Mayor Don Plusquellic announced the stadium would be built there.

Ciraldo said the project was 99 percent complete on the day we visited. More than four-hundred-thousand bricks were laid in six months, and, even so, the masonry workers took the time to add the little finishing touches that display a pride of workmanship. "We broke ground January 6, 1996, and one year and two weeks later, this is what we have," Ciraldo said.

Standing at home plate, I marveled at how short the distances between the bases seemed. Even though I knew the size of a regulation diamond, it looks bigger from the stands or on a movie or television screen.

The basepaths and the track around the field are surfaced with a compact Tennessee clay that has been topped with an orange coloring. Beneath the clay and the snow-covered grassy sod is a layered system designed to drain the field of a six-inch rain within twenty minutes, Ciraldo said. To create the system, workers removed three feet of city-dump-type fill from the stadium site and replaced it with three feet of select base fill, in which drainage ditches were dug and given structural support. A layer of pea gravel came next, then a foot of dirt, a root zone for the sod. Ciraldo called the sod and Tennessee clay "our crowning achievement."

Looking down the first base line, we realized it roughly follows what once was the towpath of the Pennsylvania & Ohio Canal, which more or less paralleled the Ohio & Erie Canal through downtown Akron before both emptied into a basin south of Exchange Street. Garden Alley had run along the towpath until the stadium construction began. Ciraldo said his workers ran into remnants of the P & O Canal when digging the foundation for Main Place at Main and Mill streets. We lamented the fact that there were no photos of that find and told Ciraldo of our research on the P & O, which began when we did our 1995 walk around the stadium site.

A map in Akron photo historian Jack Gieck's 1988 book, *A Photo Album of Ohio's Canal Era, 1825–1913,* shows the P & O entering North Main from the northeast at Tallmadge Street, which no long exists, but ran between Furnace and Market Streets. It continued along Main to a point between Mill and Quarry Streets, and then zigzagged before turning south just north of State Street. In 1995, Chuck looked east for his illustration, focusing on a view of the stadium site from the deck of the canalboat replica at Lock 2 Park. It approximated the place a photographer had stood to take a picture of a canalboat launch around the turn of the century. St. Bernard's Catholic Church was the constant on the skyline in the old canal photo and in his 1995 illustration. He also created a composite of the stadium site with the P & O running through it, based on the map in Gieck's book and an old drawing.

Someone yelled at us from one of the loges when we were at third base. It was Mike Agganis, owner of the Akron Aeros, the Indians farm team that will play its first game at Canal Park on April 10. "I'm looking for something to complain about," the owner said after greeting Ciraldo with a hug. It was his first visit since October, and he pronounced the stadium "the finest facility in the nation."

CHAPTER NINE

The Historic Role of Cemeteries

We need look no further than our cemeteries to learn much about our cities and the people who have called them home. Chuck and I knew that when we began our series, and we kept that thought in mind as we visited and revisited the final resting places of our ancestors all around Northeast Ohio.

MARCH 3, 1991

Making Connections with the Past

We embarked on our fourth year of walking around the Akron area in a familiar snow-covered setting. We began in St. Vincent's Cemetery on West Hill in 1987. Within a couple of months, we visited Glendale Cemetery, the final resting place of some of Akron's founding families, to prepare for a special Memorial Day feature. And not long after that, we climbed the nearby Glendale Steps and walked down Cadillac Hill—South Bates Street—in search of something new amid the old.

Our recent visit to Glendale Cemetery was like returning to the source, reprising an old melody at a time when our nation was engaged in a new war and our spirits were sagging. Bright sun and bitter cold combined to give every sight and sound sharpness and clarity. Somewhere in the cemetery, a plow scraped away snow that had fallen on the winding roadway the night before. We listened to the shrill calls of birds and the distant swish of West Exchange Street traffic on wet pavement.

We started near the statue of John R. Buchtel, founder of Buchtel College, which became the University of Akron. The statue stands on high ground, as does its newer twin on the Buchtel Common on the UA campus. Although the common cannot be seen from the cemetery, the Polymer Science Building at the common's western terminus shares the downtown skyline with the First National Tower and its neighbors—the city-county safety building, the twin spires of St. Bernard's Catholic Church, Canal Square YMCA, and Children's Hospital. There is a symmetry between these monuments to the living in the distance and the snow-covered monuments to the dead within the cemetery's chain-link fence.

Buchtel stands watch on an ellipse that is shared by, among other family plots, that of Ohio Columbus Barber, Ohio's match king and founder of Barberton, the scene of our February walk. We hadn't planned on making that connection. We never do. But it seems we discover a tie to the walk just completed in each new one. Barber's plot, marked with a substantial but virtually unadorned stone block, contrasts with fancier markers nearby, such as that of Charles Sumner, which contains a page of history: ". . . Born in Roxbury, Massachusetts, June 6, 1794. Settled in Middlebury, O., in 1817. Was judge of Portage Co. for nine years, and of Summit Co. from its formation until his death June 22, 1845."

Rhododendrons grow near the graves of Frank A. and Gertrude Seiberling in a miniature reprise of those they planted on the south end of Stan Hywet Hall. A simple headstone marks their graves in the same type stone as that of a tall monument that marks the family plot. A sculpted urn draped in cloth tops the spire.

Names familiar from Akron street signs and buildings graced headstones

Snow covered the statues and monuments at Glendale Cemetery.

all around us—Bartges, Sherbondy, Kenworth, Crouse, Iredell, Saalfield, Schumacher. A huge red-and-black granite rock bears the name "Lane."

Glendale Cemetery was known as Akron Rural Cemetery when it was opened in 1839. Looking to the west from the high ground, one could see through the bare trees Perkins Stone Mansion, also built at what was then the edge of town. And the former West Junior High School, built as a high school and now housing senior citizens, stood out on the western horizon.

"Majestic" best describes the vine-covered William McFarlin mausoleum.

Four columns support its roof, and bronze bars cover its double doors, also bronze.

The grave of Alvin Coe Voris looks like a miniature Washington Monument. It, too, conveys a history lesson. It speaks of a Stark County native, born in 1827, who entered the Civil War as a colonel in the 67th Ohio Volunteer Infantry and came home a major general. War was an interruption in his life, as it is today for the women and men serving in the Persian Gulf. Voris went on to serve as a Summit County Common Pleas judge from 1890 to 1896 and died on July 28, 1904.

Corporal John W. Kiely of the Sixth Ohio Battery also came home from the Civil War and lived until 1909, according to his marker, four upright cannons and a cannon ball carved from granite. That war was a permanent interruption for scores of Akron men, for whom the memorial chapel near the cemetery's entrance was built in 1875. John R. Buchtel, Colonel Simon Perkins, and George W. Crouse were among the community leaders who launched a campaign to raise $10,000 to begin its construction. It has been the scene of Memorial Day services each year since 1876, except for 1978, when repairs were being made after a sewer explosion ripped through the cemetery.

The magnificent structure, with its stained-glass windows, impressed us on our earlier visits. But it did little to lift our spirits on a day when it seemed inevitable that new names would be added to the list of war dead to be remembered at future Memorial Day services.

SEPTEMBER 17, 2000

Green Acres

Glendale Cemetery was alive with hornets and noisy birds, neither of which seemed to disturb the men who were working to restore the 125-year-old chapel. The restoration, specifically the scaffolding on the chapel and nearby belltower, caught Chuck's eye on a recent drive through the cemetery. That, coupled with a flyer for the West Hill Neighborhood Organization's second annual Victorian dinner, prompted us to take a late-summer stroll along some of its winding paths. Across the roadway from the Civil War Chapel, the stone belltower loomed over a collection of fresh tree stumps, after years of being obscured by trees. The tower's restoration began with an environmental cleanup, including the removal of three feet of pigeon droppings.

A cemetery may seem an unlikely place for a dinner party, but planners of the West Hill Neighborhood Organization's event say Glendale was a place for social events during the nineteenth century. "In the days before parks were developed, the cemetery was a great place for people to gather," says member Joan Beddell.

The cemetery dates to 1839, three years after Akron and its rival, Cascade (a.k.a. North Akron), merged and incorporated as a village. But little was done to improve what historian Karl H. Grismer termed "its natural beauty" until after the Civil War. The Cemetery Lodge near the entrance was built in 1869 with $20,000 the Ladies Cemetery Association raised by staging picnics, concerts, amateur theatrical performances, "and even a male beauty contest," Grismer wrote in *Akron and Summit County*. Industrialist John R. Buchtel won that contest and the title of Akron's most handsome man.

Buckley Post Number 12 of the Grand Army of the Republic raised $25,000 and, during 1875 and 1876 built the chapel, in which the names of Akron's Civil War veterans are inscribed on fourteen marble tablets. We couldn't see the tablets because the chapel is closed for the restoration, but we could admire up close the statue out front, which the Buckley Post erected "to our unknown dead, 1861–1865." Two gargoyles along the front roofline guard the chapel's entrance, and the words "All Honor To Our Nation's Defenders" are carved in the stone above its porch.

The chapel restoration is an ongoing project, says board member John Frank, who helped organize the Akron Civil War Memorial Society, which has raised funds to repair the roof and rehabilitate and stabilize the stonework inside and out. Frank noted, "We want the chapel to be used, at least in the warm weather."

A cannon and the Civil War Chapel are Glendale Cemetery landmarks.

We took our tour on foot and instead of searching out names of notables, we concentrated on the everyday people, such as the Spanish-American War veterans in whose memory a cannon was dedicated in 1964 by Summit County Council of the Veterans of Foreign Wars. We marveled at the dates on some of the gravestones, such as those of William and Lucinda Baldwin, who were born, respectively, in 1780 and 1787, when America was in its infancy; each lived nearly nine decades. Our last stop, on a hill overlooking a long row of mausoleums, was another reminder of the Civil War. It was the elaborate granite grave marker—four upright cannons and a cannon ball—of Corporal John W. Kiely.

AKRON CITY MAGAZINE,
JANUARY–APRIL 2004

Walking among the Guardian Angels

Her wings were clipped and part of her uplifted right arm was missing, as was her left hand. But the rest of the guardian angel was intact, staring down peacefully from the Wesener family monument on a hill in Glendale Cemetery. Nearby, Chuck was focused on another stone figure, that of a woman kneeling in prayer atop the Dunn family monument, which stands against a background of gravestones and, beyond them on the downtown Akron skyline, the YMCA Building, Children's Hospital, and the Recycle Energy plant.

But we hadn't come to study the statuary. We were there to refresh our perspective on an Akron treasure, the cemetery itself. This was our fourth visit to Glendale in fourteen years. Each visit is a reminder that a walk around Glendale Cemetery is like a continuing education course in local history. It took this visit, and a conversation with John Conti, the cemetery's general manager, to discover that Glendale was added to the National Register of Historic Places in September 2000, and that the cemetery's story is gloriously told in a new four-color brochure titled *An Historic Akron Landscape*.

And we discovered that Glendale is as contemporary as it is historic. Con-

A statue of a praying woman tops the Dunn monument at Glendale Cemetery.

ti said there were 180 new burials last year and that Glendale is far from full. The gates are open from 9 A.M. to 4 P.M. Monday through Friday. The Civil War chapel can be seen by appointment. Call 330-253-2317.

MAY 3, 1992

A Pause to Remember

If you stand facing east at State Route 18 and Medina Line Road, you might notice that the highway curves around an old cemetery. But chances are you wouldn't notice the curve or the cemetery unless they were pointed out. The curve is gentle and the cemetery small. One was created when Route 18 was widened so as not to disturb the other, the final resting place of some of the area's early settlers. No sign marks the cemetery, which is in a pine grove in Bath Township's southwest corner, just east of the Harmony Hills subdivision. Across the highway is Copley Township. A half mile to the west is Medina County, although when the land was settled, there was no Summit County, so everything in sight was in Medina. It is generally called the Miller cemetery, after the family whose private burial ground it was until Bath Township took over its maintenance. Of five cemeteries in the township, it is the only one without records of who is buried there.

There are about as many pines as there are grave markers, and the tree trunks are thicker than most, if not all, of the monuments. Many of the stone faces are so badly weathered they cannot be read. But others are legible enough to provide a sense of history, if not the whole story.

One of the first we noticed bears the legend, "In memory of Sarah F., wife of Elisha Miller. Died Aug. 17, 1858 in the 77th year of her age." William Henry Perrin's 1881 *History of Summit County* contains biographical sketches of contemporary residents. Sarah and Elisha Miller show up in the sketch on their son, Harvey, a Montrose farmer at the time Perrin was writing. The elder Millers were Connecticut natives who came to Bath in February 1827, when Harvey was nine. They owned eight hundred acres of what was then

Mysteries in Montrose

A simple inscription on a tombstone in an all-but-forgotten Copley Township cemetery sent our imaginations working overtime. At the top of the stone, in three lines, it read:

> Daniel Johnson
> died in California Feb. 13, 1851
> Age 21

Below those lines, the legend continued:

> Ester L., his wife
> died May 19, 1851
> Age 21

Was Daniel one of the thousands of adventurers lured out West by the Gold Rush of 1849? What killed him at such a tender age? Did Ester die in California, too, or did she succumb to a broken heart back here in Copley, where she mourned the loss of her young husband? We can only guess. Records for the cemetery were lost years ago.

Daniel and Ester Johnson are buried in a fenced-in, well-tended half acre or so surrounded by the ever-growing commercial mecca at State Route 18 and Cleveland-Massillon Road. The juxtaposition of the tiny burial plot on Cleveland-Massillon Road, with its crop of weathered headstones leaning in every direction, and the newness of everything around it, inspired us to take a closer look.

Reading inscriptions on tombstones is fun and often informative. Our wives think we spend too much time gazing at grave markers, but we've never visited a cemetery without finding a good story or picture. This tiny cemetery was no exception. It's nestled between Copley's Fire Station No. 2 and the Roadhouse restaurant, and across from the Cleveland-Massillon Road en-

The Henry Hurlbut monument stands in the cemetery in Montrose.

trance to Rosemont Commons. It was a perfect day for a walk outdoors—cloudy but with plenty of sun to brighten the fall colors on the low-lying brush in the field that borders the cemetery's south and west sides.

The U.S. and Ohio flags outside the fire station, attached to their riggings only by the top corner of the Stars and Stripes, blew erratically in a stiff wind. Thick berry vines covered one corner of the cemetery's chain-link fence, and its gate was tied shut with rope.

A circular concrete-and-metal U.S. Geological Survey marker about ten inches in diameter was embedded in the grass just inside the cemetery's southeast corner. It marked the elevation at 1016 feet above sea level. Next to it was a salmon-colored post advising all who read it not to disturb the marker. There were no other signs, either identifying the cemetery or inviting us to come in or stay out, so we decided to stop at the fire station before entering. Firefighter John Gordon told us the cemetery is open to the public and gave us a telephone number for Jim Welton, the cemetery sexton.

Instead of looking at the Montrose area from within the cemetery, as had been our plan, we decided to look first at the cemetery as seen by the thousands who flock to the area daily to shop and dine. We walked west along Brookwall Drive, a short access road between Cleveland-Massillon and Brookmont Roads. To our left, behind the fire station, was a field with weeds so tall they all but hid the cemetery. Litter was strewn along the curb—there is no sidewalk—and just beyond. Soft-drink containers. Fast-food boxes and wrappers. Even a pair of jockey shorts! To our right were three large Dumpsters at the back entrances of a restaurant and a row of shops. In fact, from that perspective, the whole shopping strip looked like Dumpster Heaven. It must have been trash-collection day, because several trash-hauling trucks drove by during our walk around the block, and we concluded that at least some of the litter we saw might have fallen from those trucks.

As we approached the corner of Brookwall and Brookmont, we saw a small building that looked like an old shed. When we got there, it turned out to be a relatively new cinderblock utility building—no doubt serving the commercial strip, the Chambrel residential community on Brookmont, or both.

Looking east from Brookmont, we could see the tops of the Roadhouse restaurant and the buildings at Rosemont Commons over the weeds—thistles, goldenrod, and other flora, the names of which I'll never know or remember. Flowering sweet peas grew in abundance along the edge of the field, and two giant bumblebees flitted among them. A woman was picking wildflowers, and another woman was feeding the ducks in the pond by Chambrel.

To our right, on the south side of Bywood Road, were two houses. Each was now home to a commercial enterprise—the Akron Montessori School and Rose Victoria, a Victorian gift shop. To our left, we found the most glorious view of the field in early autumn. Everything was reaching for the sky—remnants of spiky yellow blooms, wild daisies, and a blood-red plant that glowed in the sunlight.

We admired the long border of spruce trees on Bywood near Cleveland-Massillon and the rhododendron that proliferated on the front lawn of the house at the intersection's southwest corner. And then we were back at the cemetery gate. The rope untied easily, and we were soon reading snippets of Copley Township history.

Joseph Hawkins was buried there in 1818 at age eighty-nine, his marker reported. That means he was born in 1729, forty-seven years before the colonies declared their independence from Great Britain. We don't know where he was born or when he came to the Western Reserve, but we know it was early in its history.

We jotted down pages of names and dates, hoping to flesh out some of these stories—especially the one about Daniel and Ester Johnson—when we spoke to the sexton. However, the records of the cemetery and another small and equally old plot on Hametown Road were lost years ago, Welton reported. He is in charge of maintaining both cemeteries and a third, larger one on Copley Road just west of the circle.

Welton, who grew up on the family farm on Route 18 where Interstate 77 crosses it, was able to unravel the mystery of why some of the tombstones face the front of the cemetery and some face the rear. Burials followed no pattern or routine in the early days, he said. People piled rocks on top of the coffins before filling in the graves and later erected markers. That's why so many of the old stones lean in all directions. The sexton said he is taking bids on a project to build real foundations for the markers so they won't lean or fall over.

FEBRUARY 1, 1998

Where History Blooms

A floral arrangement, dried by the elements, led us to the spot we were looking for on the north side of the snow-covered Erie Cemetery on East Ninth Street across from Jacobs Field in downtown Cleveland. The flowers, displayed on a green wire stand, were placed at the grave of John Malvin last November when a small group of men and women gathered to dedicate a marker where none had been since the Cleveland abolitionist and civil rights pioneer died in 1880.

We had read a newspaper account about the ceremony and brought along the clipping, which included a photo, in the hope we could find the marker. Still, we were surprised the flowers were still there. That was just one of the pleasant surprises that greeted Chuck and me on my first and his second walk through the cemetery. I'm embarrassed to admit I had planned to explore the cemetery since the day I discovered it forty-two years ago Friday (February 6) on my first day of work at the *Cleveland Press*. Why, I had asked one of my colleagues, do they call it the Erie Street Cemetery? Ninth Street was originally called Erie Street, I learned. The word "street" was dropped from the cemetery's name sometime in the years since 1956, but I had never taken the time to walk the ten-acre plot that was described as "far out of town" when Cleveland city fathers bought it in 1827 to replace the city's first burial ground at Ontario Street and Prospect Avenue.

Fast-forward to last fall. I had parked my car in the Hanna parking deck at East 14th Street and Prospect on my way to an interview when the ceme-

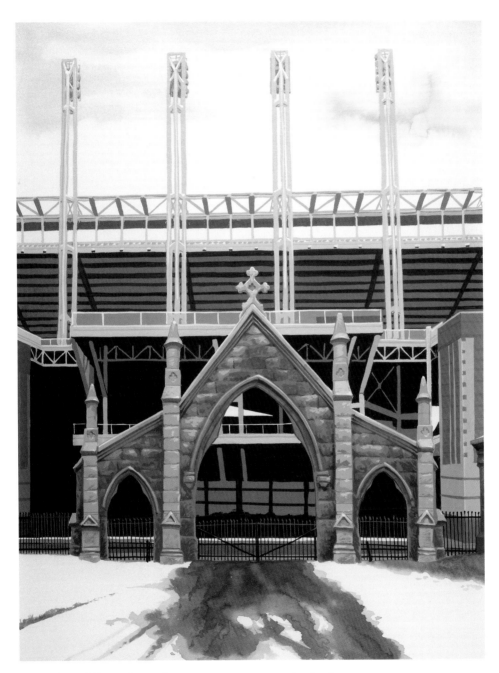

Jacobs Field looms beyond Erie Cemetery gate in Cleveland.

tery caught my eye. Looking down from one of the upper parking levels, I was treated to a panorama that I'd never appreciated before and which placed Jacobs Field, one of the city's newest landmarks, in a context with some of its oldest.

To the southwest, the twin spires of St. Maron's Catholic Church peeked over the top of the former Brownell School (later Cuyahoga Community College's first home and now a branch of Capital University) on Sumner Court, on the cemetery's south side. Brownell, one of Cleveland's oldest schools, counted among its students industrialist Marcus A. Hanna, playwright and poet Langston Hughes, and Olympic gold medalist Jesse Owens.

West and north of the cemetery, the five-story, castlelike tower of the 105-year-old Grays Armory rose above the roofline of a Goodyear service center. And beyond Grays loomed Ameritech's art deco, green-topped office tower at 750 Huron Road, which was built as the corporate headquarters of the former Ohio Bell Telephone Company and is thought by many to have been the prototype for the building housing the *Daily Planet* in the *Superman* comics.

It was time to visit the cemetery, I decided. Chuck agreed when I proposed it, then came up with the newspaper clipping about the ceremony honoring the memory of John Malvin. All we had to do was find the new marker.

Mike Carlo, supervisor of Cleveland's ten cemeteries, said the main gate on Ninth Street is padlocked most of the time but that the East 14th Street entrance would be open, and it was. The cemetery is bisected by an unpaved roadway wide enough for two cars. As good as the panorama was from the parking deck, the view of downtown Cleveland from within the cemetery was even better. North of the cemetery wall looms the sixteen-story Renaissance on Playhouse Square office tower, opened in 1990 and home to Star Bank, among other tenants.

Chuck was taken by the similarity of shapes on both sides of the wall. It was as if someone had the cemetery's pyramid-topped gravestones in mind when the office building was being designed. These shapes and the golden reflections of the clouds in the building's glass exterior prompted one of today's illustrations. The other illustration was inspired by the cathedrallike appearance of Jacobs Field when viewed through the cemetery's main entrance.

For the first time I realized how much more there was to Grays Armory than the "castle" that fronts on Bolivar Road. From within the cemetery, we saw that the armory stretched back a block to Erie Court in two additional buildings.

Starting at the East 14th end of the cemetery, we soon realized, was like walking backwards through time. The grave markers got older as we walked west toward Ninth.

Cars visible in the newspaper photo helped us guess correctly that Malvin's grave was on the north side of the cemetery and possibly midway between 14th and Ninth. That was the easy part, thanks to the roadway where the cars were parked. The tough job was approximating where the photographer had been standing because so little of the world beyond the cemetery remained in the photo once it was cropped.

I read grave markers while Chuck concentrated on discovering the photographer's vantage point, and just as he announced that he thought he had found it I spotted the green stand and its withered display. We hurried across the snow to find, at the base of the stand, the ice-covered, two-by-one-foot marker. We cleared it to read the engraving, which, according to the newspaper account, came from Malvin's obituary on August 2, 1880: "The eventful career and noble work of a worthy man whose thoughts were of his people, John Malvin, accomplished educator, ship owner, minister and carpenter."

The Dictionary of Cleveland Biography, compiled by David D. Van Tassel and John J. Grabowski, told us more about Malvin, who came to Cleveland by way of Cincinnati in 1831 at age thirty-six. The native of Prince William County, Virginia, was the son of a white mother and slave father and, therefore, considered free. This enabled him to learn to read but did not protect him from the same corporal punishment inflicted on slaves when he entered the work force.

Malvin worked as a cook and carpenter, operated a sawmill, and was a canalboat captain. He was also a Baptist minister who became a charter member of the First Baptist Church, which was built on land where the Terminal Tower now stands. He is credited with preventing the segregation of members at worship. Malvin also raised his voice in opposition to segregated schools in Cleveland and throughout the state. In 1832, he organized a committee that provided schools for black children denied education in white schools, and by 1848 his efforts led to the Ohio Legislature's abolishment of a state law limiting public school access to white children only. Before the Civil War, he lectured on behalf of the Ohio Anti-Slavery Society and reportedly was active in the Underground Railroad. When the war began, he helped organize a black company that joined the 54th and 55th Massachusetts Regiments.

Standing at his grave, surrounded by the graves of so many other early residents of Cleveland, we couldn't help but marvel at this old—but new to us—chapter in history.

But there was more. Across the roadway and slightly to the west of Malvin's grave, we spotted a large rock with printing etched into its surface. At its base were four small U.S. flags and two plastic milk jugs with more withered flowers projecting from the narrow necks. And neatly bordered and carefully set into the soil in nine pieces was the wreckage of an older tombstone. This was the grave of Joc-o-Sot, who, the inscription told us, was "The Walking Bear, a distinguished chief" who was a member of the Osaukee tribe and was wounded in the Black Hawk War. A metal plaque on the other side of the rock described Joc-o-Sot as the Indian ambassador to President John Tyler. William Ganson Rose's book *Cleveland: The Making of a City* called him "Cleveland's most famous Indian," and reported he succumbed to the lingering effects of his war injury in 1844 at age thirty-four.

Joc-o-Sot and John Malvin came to Cleveland around the same time. The Indian was a friend of Dr. Horace A. Ackley, with whom he hunted and fished. He joined a touring theatrical troupe to earn money for his tribe and became a sensation in England. Queen Victoria, to whom he was presented, commissioned a full-length portrait of him. The broken tombstone, according to another marker, was preserved after vandals smashed it in 1907.

Near the Ninth Street end of the cemetery, we found the plot containing the original sixteen graves moved to Erie Street from the original cemetery on Ontario in 1826—a year before the ten-acre cemetery was officially created. A marker placed in 1948 by the Early Settlers Association listed the names of the deceased, although many were unknown.

We also found the grave of David Eldridge, the Connecticut Land Company surveyor who drowned in the Grand River in June 1797 and was the first white person buried in the Ontario cemetery in what was then the year-old Western Reserve town of Cleveland.

Just inside the Ninth Street entrance, a well-worn stone brought us back to the beginning. It marks the grave of Rebekah Carter, who died August 14, 1803, seven years after her parents, Lorenzo and Rebekah Carter, became the first white settlers of Cleveland, living in a cabin on the east bank of the Cuyahoga River. Her parents are buried in the cemetery, too, as is Cleveland's first mayor, John W. Willey, although we didn't search for those graves. A surveyor, a white pioneer child, an Indian chief, and a black freedom fighter seemed to say it all for us, at least for this walk through time.

AUGUST 3, 1997

Fresh Face on Main Street

All we needed was some theme music, perhaps Dave Loggins's 1974 hit "Please Come to Boston," as we strolled along Main Street in this tiny hamlet, named for a city in England, not the one in Massachusetts. We came to see a new log home, the first new construction in Boston in recent memory, and the old cemetery that bears the hamlet's name. Both are on the north end of Main, a short street never intended to be any longer.

People have been coming to Boston in droves since the Ohio & Erie Canal towpath was reopened in Summit and Cuyahoga Counties and the 161-year-old trapezoid-shaped Boston Store was restored and turned into a canal museum by the National Park Service. Chuck and I have been among the visitors, but we hadn't ever walked the streets of Boston. It took a glimpse of the log home last month to remind me of our sin of omission.

Our first stop was the old frame house that stands behind the M.D. Garage, a landmark of more recent vintage than the Boston Store. The house is used as office space by Jeff Winstel, park service historian and planner, who wasn't there when we came to call. At a glance, the M.D. Garage—so identified in white letters on a black background that stretches across the top of the building—looks like an operational service station and has fooled more than one visitor. A big, round blue-and-white sign above the gas pump island told us to "Be Sure With Pure." (Gasoline was priced at 26.9 cents and 29.9 cents a gallon; diesel was 20.9 cents a gallon.) A small sign over the door bears the name Marjan Dzerzynski and the words "Pure Products." We peeked through windows in the front and rear of the building. It was empty except for a tractor and old rocking chair.

A woman called to us from across the road, saying she had old photos of the station and other Boston scenes of yesteryear in her store, Grandma's Watering Hole, and she did. Mary Boodey gave us a short course in Boston history since 1945, when she and her husband, the late Rollin Boodey, bought the store from Norman Wise. She also told us Marjan is pronounced as if the "J" were an "I," and that the log home is being built by Skip Ausperk. We admired the snowball bushes in the yard of her home next door, and she said, "Yeah, and the deer like 'em, too. They eat everything." Boodey's home stands at the northeast corner of Boston Mills Road and Main Street.

The northwest corner is vacant of buildings, but a sign advises that a house at 581 Main is for sale. Also owned by Ausperk, whose given name is Charles, it stands next to the new house at the north end of the street, near the cemetery entrance. Ausperk wasn't there when we arrived, so I called later and spoke to his wife, Lisa, who said they bought the house at 581 Main for the one-and-one-half acres it stands on, with the intention of building a new house. It is not a tiny log cabin, but rather a two-story dwelling along the lines of Ben Cartwright's ranch house on the TV show *Bonanza*. The Ausperks live in a smaller home nearby on Riverview Road. It's owned by the park service,

Boston Cemetery is a lesson in local history.

she said, which was not enthusiastic about their plans to build on Main Street. Her husband's father, also named Charles Ausperk, owned the Riverview Inn, which once stood where a bridge abutment for Interstate 271 now stands.

A large gray stone marking the graves of the elder Charles Ausperk and his wife, the former Ruth Stine, was one of the first things we saw when we walked into the cemetery. It is near the base of the flat-topped hill that contains most of the graves. From our vantage point (in the cemetery's center), we could understand why the earliest settlers—and, according to many accounts we've heard, the Indians before them—chose this place to bury their dead. The hill rises sharply out of the flood plain, which is not disturbed by any man-made structure for miles to the north. The Stanford family monument, decorated with a small U.S. flag at its base, is the tallest in the cemetery and stands near its center. James Stanford is credited with being Boston's first settler, in 1806. The road named for the family is open between Boston Mills Road and the hostel that was established in the old Stanford family homestead.

Looking west from the center of the cemetery, we could see the snowmaking apparatus at the top of the hill at the Boston Mills ski resort. We found graves of several members of the Jaite family, which gave its name to the hamlet that became the park service headquarters at Riverview and Vaughn Roads. The earliest burial we discovered was that of John Thompson, who, according to the marker, died August 24, 1819, "in the 76th year of his life." It was one of those "wow!" moments. Thompson, we figured, was already thirty-three when the Declaration of Independence was signed.

A small stone marked only with the name "James Brown" provided another thrill. Brown was legendary in these parts as a counterfeiter who served a stretch in a Louisiana jail for attempting to smuggle $1.5 million in bogus bucks out of the port of New Orleans in the 1830s. Tales of Brown's adventures were passed along by word of mouth long before anyone wrote them down. Chuck and I first heard about Brown from our friend Joe Jesensky, who had made the Cuyahoga Valley a life's study. A 1932 account in the *Akron*

Times-Press credited Brown, his brother Dan, and a friend named William G. Taylor with engineering "the most gigantic counterfeiting plot in history. . . . Dan died in jail. Jim returned to Boston, a popular hero, and was elected justice of the peace. He lived to plan many more counterfeiting coups, but died from a fall into the hold of a canal boat. Jim's grave, marked by a headstone, now grows the best roses in Boston cemetery."

There were no roses the day we visited, but the marker was the same one shown in a photo that accompanied the *Times-Press* story.

MARCH 12, 2000

A Sense of Wander

The family name—Quirk—was one of the few legible words on the time-worn tombstone in the St. Vincent Catholic Cemetery on West Market Street, next to and behind the Tangier restaurant in Akron's West Hill neighborhood. The stone caught our eye because someone had augmented the carved letters and numbers with paint that had not weathered well. To the east, beyond the family marker, we looked through a residential neighborhood at the downtown Akron skyline. This was the view Chuck was looking for. It had that almost-spring look of a grimy world just waiting for the rain to fall after a late-winter thaw.

We visited the cemetery in morning so the sun—if it poked through the clouds—would be in the east. The visit reprises our first, thirteen years ago this month, when we invited readers to join us—figuratively—on a walk along West Market between Balch Street and Rhodes Avenue. To our delight, many readers accepted and have been—figuratively—tramping around the five-county Akron area with us once a month ever since. Two readers interpreted the invitation literally. One woman wrote to inquire where she should meet us for our April 1987 walk. She was serious. Through it all, we never failed to discover something new about even the most familiar places we visited.

The St. Vincent Cemetery dates to at least 1854. It is bordered by the hustle-bustle of West Market just outside its fence to the north and the residen-tial neighborhood beyond the fence to the south. Crosby Street runs behind the cemetery, and its homes have large backyards, we discovered. We were looking down on the yards because the cemetery is on much higher ground, except for the rear portion, which slopes to a debris-filled ditch.

Just before the slope, we found three large wooden crosses, replicating those on Calvary, and at the base of one, a small American flag. If these cross-es were there thirteen years ago, we didn't remember them. Nearby, along the high ground, was a plot marked with three tiny handmade crosses. We won-dered if it were a plot at all or, perhaps, the work of neighborhood children.

Another new feature, to us at least, was a small stone marker in the center of the cemetery, where the driveway begins to form a circle. The marker, adorned with a rosary, represents lives that never were because of abortion.

As much as we have enjoyed the discovery aspect of our travels, the great-est enrichment has been what readers have shared in letters and phone calls after we've presented our pedestrian perspectives. After we visited Akron's Mason Park last year, Richard Ross of Tallmadge wrote about walking there en route to Mason Elementary School in the late 1930s. "However, it wasn't Mason Park in those days," Ross wrote. "It was called the Clay Pits. As the story goes, they were digging clay with a steam shovel and they struck a spring and the pit filled with water up to the (shovel's) metal roof. We neighbor-hood kids used to go skinny-dipping. We used to dive in and swim out to the steam shovel, climb on the roof and dive off. It scares me to think about it to-day. Several kids drowned or were injured diving from the edge of the pit."

A letter from Wendell A. Scott of Akron in 1989 came with illustra-tions—copies of six pencil sketches Scott had made in the 1930s of the rail yard at the west end of Eastwood Avenue just before it terminates at North Street and Home Avenue. Scott's letter was inspired by Chuck's illustration of the rail yard that appeared in the magazine on January 4, 1989. "I made friends," Scott wrote of one sketch. "One of the machinists was [a] self-appointed sign maker. I made this sketch as he was working on a drive sign. One man remarked, 'The kid is making a picture of Bill.' His buddy replied,

'What is he using?'" The answer, unprintable in a family newspaper, was "earthy humor," Scott concluded.

Elizabeth Brooks Laurenson of North Canton devoted two single-spaced typewritten pages to a reminiscence about growing up in her family home, built around 1916, at Orchard Road and Mull Avenue in Akron after our 1995 story about Shady Park.

"Orchard Road was a short street that connected Mull Avenue to West Market," she wrote. "The area had been an old apple orchard, and apple trees still abounded in this new residential area. I was born in 1918 and this was the house I grew up in. We referred to the rutted, unimproved extension of Mull to West Exchange Street as 'the bumpy road.' Motorized vehicles traversed it at their peril. All of that property now belongs to Rockynol, but in our growing up years that whole beautiful property, bounded by West Exchange, Mull Avenue, Putnam Road on the east, and Our Lady of the Elms convent and school on the west was known as the Adams estate, where the wealthy owner lived in lonely but magnificent splendor."

It would be difficult to top that last phrase, so we'll end this story as we ended the first one: If you enjoyed our stroll, perhaps you'll join us next month for another.

CHAPTER TEN

Exploring Cities and Towns beyond Akron

Our travels were generally limited to Summit, Portage, Medina, Stark, and Wayne Counties during the years Chuck and I presented the products of our pedestrian pursuits to readers of the Beacon Journal *because those five counties were where the newspaper based its circulation. We found no dearth of fascinating places, large and small, as what follows demonstrates.*

MAY 7, 1989

Hiking by Hale

When Hale Farm and Village opens for the season, visitors will find a new building on the southwest corner of the Western Reserve Village Green. It is the reconstructed Jonathan E. Herrick House, which has resembled a large pile of sandstone rubble for the last seven years. We got a sneak preview of the new attraction on a springtime walk along a mile of country road that winds between Hale Farm and the Everett Road covered bridge.

Wooden steps lead down to the water on either side of Furnace Run. The water level was low for spring, thanks to the mild winter. Instead of rushing past us, as it might have after a heavy snow melt, the stream was all but still until wind gusts created exotic patterns on the surface. It was here that flood-waters flattened the original, nearly hundred-year-old bridge in 1975, leaving Summit County without a covered bridge for the next decade. Construction of a replica, undertaken by the National Park Service, was completed in 1986.

Oak Hill Road is all S-curves between the bridge and the farm, but the traffic was light, making for safe and easy walking. In that short distance, we were in three communities—Boston Township, Cuyahoga Falls, and Bath—all within the Cuyahoga Valley National Recreation Area.

We heard Hale Farm before we saw it. That is, we heard the *baaing* before we rounded a bend and saw a small herd of black-faced sheep grazing in a field across the road from the reconstructed Village Green. Two horses in an adjoining field were the only other livestock in view. But we didn't come to see livestock.

Herrick House, which was dismantled and moved, stone by stone, from its original site on Darrow Road in Twinsburg in 1981, was our destination.

Kevin Grocot, carpenter and mason at Hale Farm, and helper Mike Lenz were laying a course of stone near the roofline when we arrived. Architect Nicholas G. Popa of Bath, the construction manager, and electrician Blair Maynard were conferring in the muddy field below. Popa said the crew should be working on the roof by early May. Wood shingles characteristic of 1845, when Herrick House was originally built, will be used there. Work began in the fall of 1987 with the foundation, Popa said, and the first course of stone was laid in April 1988.

Herrick House is one of the few Greek Revival homes made of stone in the Western Reserve, according to Hale Farm superintendent Siegfried Buerling. It was recorded in measured drawings and photos by the National Park Service's Historic American Buildings Survey in 1936 and listed in 1974 in the National Register of Historic Places.

The family of Oscar Ross, its last residential owner, offered it to the Western Reserve Historical Society in 1975, but because it was in no danger

The historic Herrick House, dismantled and moved from Twinsburg, was reconstructed at Hale Farm and Village in 1989.

of being destroyed, society officials declined the offer, in keeping with its policy of not moving buildings if they can be saved in their original locations. The family sold the property to a commercial developer but insisted on a deed restriction that called for the developer to give the Historical Society three months to remove the house if demolition was considered. The Historical Society exercised its option in 1981 after the developer announced plans to demolish Herrick House to make room for an industrial park. National Park Service architect Norma Stefanik, then a graduate student in architecture, developed a numbering system for the stones and made field drawings of the house before it was dismantled.

Popa took us inside Herrick House to see sights the public never will within its twenty-inch-wide walls. The interior stone facing and rough timbers—many of them original—will be covered by walls and ceilings. We felt like boys playing in a fortress. In fact, when Chuck came down the ladder from the second floor, he commented: "It's just like my old days of wearing a coonskin cap. It's like being in the Alamo."

Tourists won't have that opportunity. But they will be able to visit a replica of a typical nineteenth-century Western Reserve cheese-producing farm. Herrick House had four rooms upstairs and four down, plus a summer kitchen that was added later. The house will be the nucleus of the dairy farm complex. A replica of the summer kitchen will be used as a cheese shop. Completing the complex will be the restored Hale Farm barn and a springhouse moved from North Bloomfield. But that's a season away. This year's tourists will see the finishing touches added, such as the antique mortar that will be applied to the rear of Herrick House, where modern block was used on a portion of the wall.

MARCH 2, 1997

Sweet Celebration

Thin columns of smoke rose above the treeline as we drove along Oak Hill Road in Bath Township. The smoke was coming from the chimneys of the sugarhouse and sawmill at Hale Farm and Village. It was early on the first day of Maple Sugaring Days, Hale Farm's annual celebration of the pioneer craft of making maple syrup, but the parking lot was already filling up with carloads of families who wanted to see the process and sample the product.

Granular snow fell from gray clouds as Chuck and I hiked to the gatehouse through which all visitors must pass. The air was cold—too cold for this to be a good day for collecting sap from the map trees, Barbara Byler, Hale Farm's special program manager, told us. The previous day had been unseasonably warm and the sap had flowed better. Sap rises when the weather is warm and falls back toward the roots when the temperature drops, so cold nights and warm days are the optimum conditions for the collection process, Byler said. On this cold day, only one sap collection was scheduled, at 1 P.M. On a good flow day, a sledge or wagon pulled by a team of oxen makes the rounds of the sugar maples at 11 A.M. and 2 P.M.

In the sugarhouse, the sap is boiled to become, through evaporation, maple sugar. The sugarbush is a grove of maples where up to 180 buckets are hung from 120 trees, and where Hale Farm workers demonstrate the process as practiced by the early settlers.

We came prepared to walk in mud because of the recent thaw, but except for some rutted wheel tracks on the path that looped the sugarbush, the ground was relatively hard and dry.

Byler showed us how to remove the cover of a metal sap bucket that hung beneath a spigot near the base of a maple near the gatehouse. The sap inside was about four inches deep, colorless, clear, and covered by a thin layer of ice. Other buckets we examined along the path to the sugarhouse contained about as much of the ice-covered liquid. The path took us past the sawmill and the largest sawdust pile I have ever seen, and two tree stumps that were taller than my five-and-a-half-foot height.

We crossed the wooden footbridge over Hale Run and headed across a carpet of last autumn's leaves toward a lean-to in the middle of the sugarbush. There, volunteer Bob Firis of Wadsworth was cooking sap in a pot hanging over a campfire on a contraption of a style dating to the days when Indians taught the settlers to make maple sugar. The contraption consisted of a long pole made from a tree branch about four inches in diameter, an upright Y-shaped log in which the bucket end of the pole was cradled, and another upright to which the other end of the pole could be anchored at various heights to control the bucket's distance from the flames. Firis explained the process to visitors, then let a youngster in the crowd try on the wooden yoke from which two buckets could be hung for carrying. When full of syrup, each bucket weighs twenty-five pounds, Firis said.

We returned to the early twentieth century inside the sugarhouse, where Hale Farm educator Mike Winter and farm worker Eric Hunter explained syrup making as practiced by settler Jonathan Hale's grandson, C.O. Hale, until his death in 1938. The atmosphere was smoky from the wood fire and steamy from the large steel evaporator in which the sap was cooking. Steel evaporators replaced those made of copper in 1930, Hunter said. The tiny building's cupola is designed to let the smoke and steam escape, while keeping out the rain.

It is possible, in theory, to produce a gallon of syrup per tree, but that rarely happens, Hunter said. Only two and a half gallons had been produced by February 22, when Maple Sugaring Days began, and Hale Farm's expectation for the season ranged from thirty to fifty gallons.

Hunter shared an anecdote about a man who tapped his own maple trees and tried making maple syrup at home and, for his trouble, loosened and collapsed the plaster in his kitchen ceiling. It takes fifty gallons of sap boiling for five hours to make one gallon of syrup, Hunter said. You can do that at home, he said, but suggested boiling small amounts at a time and doing so outdoors.

At our breakfast of pancakes, link sausage, and Hale Farm syrup, we were

Steam rises from the sugarhouse at Hale Farm and Village.

serenaded by guitarist Eileen Rohr of Canal Fulton and hammer dulcimerist Tim Darnell of Massillon, who played a Scots folk tune, "The Water is Wide."

Hale Farm marketing coordinator Jim Brazytis gave us a reason to come back soon with news that interior restoration is nearing completion at Herrick House. Cheesemaking and butter-churning have been demonstrated in a back section of the house for at least five years, so we were surprised to learn that the restoration project wasn't completed. Brazytis said Herrick House will reopen with a bit of fanfare on July 4.

OCTOBER 1, 1995

Crossing the Circle

Connecticut Yankees surveyed and settled the Western Reserve, so it was no surprise to learn that the historic First Congregational Church has a twin in Litchfield, Connecticut. What we found surprising was that the Tallmadge church—the building, not the congregation—is older than the one in Litchfield. We learned all this after taking a walk inside the circle, which is really an oval on land the early settlers of Tallmadge called the public square.

We are always on the lookout for unfamiliar views of the familiar, and Tallmadge Circle certainly qualified. Few of the thousands who drive around it every day are likely ever to park their cars and step inside. It just isn't thought of as a destination. But it wasn't always that way. Historical markers at the church and the old town hall reveal that the circle was *the* destination for matters of church and state for many years.

The church came first, soon after the Reverend David Bacon bought the township's twelve thousand acres—6,245 from Benjamin Tallmadge of Litchfield and the rest from Ephraim Starr of Goshen, Connecticut—and came to the Ohio wilderness to establish a Congregational community in 1807. Bacon named the township for Tallmadge, who was the son of a Congregational minister, a lieutenant colonel in the American army during the

The old town hall, seen across the Tallmadge Circle, was built in 1859.

Revolutionary War, a member of the U.S. Congress, and a secret service agent for President George Washington.

A booklet prepared by congregation members Joan Haby and Nancy Beken for the church's one-hundred-and-seventieth anniversary (August 20, 1995) reports the that first services were held in the first log cabin built in the township. The booklet quotes Bacon's plans for Tallmadge: "The section in the center of the township is to be left for the institution of the community. . . . the Church and the Town Hall. The parsonage, school, library, shops and residences of shop keepers [*sic*] are to face the Public Square."

Roads sixty-six-feet wide were surveyed to run north, northeast, east, southeast, south, southwest, west, and northwest, like spokes from the hub of a giant wheel.

In 1821, an Ohio Historical Society marker told us, local landowners provided the timber to build the church that stands on the circle today. The church was, the marker said, "designed and constructed by one of Ohio's first architects, Col. Lemuel Porter. Dedicated on Sept. 8, 1825, the structure is considered to be a perfect example of the pure Connecticut-type of Federal architecture."

The town hall dates to 1859, a Tallmadge Historical Society marker informed us, and its second floor was the fifth home of the Tallmadge Academy, which was started in 1815 and "served students from Northeast Ohio who desired advanced courses not offered by school systems until 1876." That building, too, is of the Federal design, but what appear to be four columns on the front of the building are in fact decorative trim. The church's columns—four on the front and two on a side porch—are real. The town hall replaced one that had stood on the northeast corner of the circle and North Avenue. The Tallmadge Historical Society was established on March 24, 1858 in the older hall. The society boasts of being Ohio's oldest. The 1859 town hall was also home to the Tallmadge Police Department until a new station was built on Northeast Avenue in 1980.

We crisscrossed the circle's interior on sidewalks that don't follow the orderly pattern of the spokelike avenues. Park benches dotted the landscape, including several new ones manufactured in Akron by the Plastic Lumber Company. The Stars and Stripes, Ohio's red, white, and blue pennant, and a banner for service personnel missing in action were flying on one staff above the Tallmadge Veterans Memorial, which includes a peace marker in English and three other languages. The marker was a 1988 gift from pupils of Munroe Elementary School.

We found two natural features as interesting as the buildings. One is a large weathered boulder inscribed "Centennial 1889" and said to be on the exact center of Tallmadge Township. The other is a tall silver maple near the front of the church. The tree is nearly five feet in diameter, clearly the oldest on the circle, and we could not help but wonder if it might not have been a sapling when Lemuel Porter was building the church.

In the end, it was the church that fascinated us most. The markers said it was the oldest Ohio church continuously occupied as a place of worship. That's technically true. Community Easter morning and Thanksgiving eve services are held in the church, and it is frequently used for wedding ceremonies. But the last regular service was held on May 11, 1969, a day before the congregation moved to its present home at 85 Heritage Drive in Tallmadge.

The old church faces south. Its front steps and sidewalk were covered with birdseed that had been used to shower the bride and groom at a recent wedding. Looking up, we admired the detailed design, diamonds within squares, on the eaves, the working weathervane atop the steeple, and the six-foot shutters on ancient hinges on each side of twenty side windows. The windows must be a washer's nightmare. Each has forty panes. That's four hundred on the east wall and four hundred on the west.

The deed to the historic church was transferred to the Ohio Historical Society in 1971. The church was placed on the National Register of Historic Places in 1933.

AUGUST 4, 1996

Strolling Hudson Green

A tall young businessman strolled down the sidewalk chatting on his cellular phone. A woman drove by in a Mercedes, chauffeuring two Scotties, one black and one white. Very upscale. Very Nineties. Very Hudson. It was the middle of a hot summer day, and Chuck and I were standing in the shade of a large oak tree at East Main and Division Streets in Hudson, a couple of miles from where we intended to be. The O'Brien Cemetery on Hudson Drive was our original destination, but a "Keep Out" sign suggested we save that walk for another time—when and if we had permission to venture beyond its gates.

It was time, we decided, to take a close-up look at the Hudson Green and the streets leading away from it. We had avoided the green as being too obviously Hudson when we walked around town five years ago. Driving through

Hudson twice a day for years had led me to believe I had seen everything there was to see around the green. That myth dissolved as soon as we parked the car. The first new thing I learned was that the name of the street on the east side of the green, paralleling Main Street, is East Main Street.

The commercial strip of Main Street between Streetsboro and Owen Brown Streets was just a block to the west, but it seemed less touristy from the shade of the oak. In fact, from that distance we might have been in Anytown, U.S.A. Any small town, that is, with so many buildings displaying historical markers that I abandoned any idea of recording every detail. A dental practice occupies what was identified as the former Ellsworth Store at Division and East Main; the pale yellow-and-white-brick building dates to 1841. Its neighbors date to 1891 and 1824, according to the markers.

Hudson's city hall stands at the northeast corner of Church and East Main. The two-story beige brick structure has two towers on the front, and it is still identified as "Hudson Town Hall" in the sandstone arch above the front door. That's the familiar view, the one transient motorists are likely to remember.

Anyone who takes the time to stop and walk around the corner will see the view Chuck chose for his first illustration—the rear of the building, which has a belltower on its roof and originally housed the fire department, according to the sandstone marker above the arched green double doors. The marker also dates the building to 1896, just ninety-nine years after David Hudson of Goshen, Connecticut, and two partners bought the land that would become Hudson Township.

The Johnson-Romito Funeral Home is in a sprawling former residence at the southeast corner of Church and East Main. The building is magnificent, with wraparound porches and gingerbread. Chuck resisted the temptation to focus on the front, choosing instead to sketch the gingerbread on the back of the building and that along the roofline of the building next door.

The Hudson seen by motorists was forgotten as we walked east on Church Street. We weren't alone. We counted three moms pushing strollers and one woman walking her dog in the short time it took to get around the

A woman walking her dog, flowers in bloom, and a stained glass window were three images captured on the Hudson Green.

block. Workers were reroofing a neat little house in the middle of the block. It also had a wraparound porch. Another home, painted a lovely green, had a gorgeous front yard flower garden with a gazing ball on a pedestal at its center. What's a gazing ball? It's a mirrored globe strategically placed to reflect its surroundings. I'd seen them before but had never heard of the term until that day. Chuck said he stumbled upon the term while researching something else. The same house had a backyard as interesting as the front, with an old-fashioned gasoline pump on display in front of the garage.

Looking back from the corner of Church and College Streets, we couldn't see Main Street anymore. We might have been in a small town in Connecticut.

Next to the Hudson Masonic Lodge on Streetsboro at College was a find that defined the premise of all of our walks. Two pink roses grew at the corner of a front yard that is screened from the bustle of traffic on Streetsboro—the busy State Route 303—by a wooden fence and dense shrubbery. We peered over the fence and noted the roses grew in a well-tended plot but were not even visible to the people who planted them because of the shrubs. You might say they were there for the benefit of anyone who took the time to notice. They grew so close to the sidewalk that we could have picked them. But instead we simply enjoyed their fragrance and moved on.

Orange and yellow lilies abounded in the yard next door to the former Catholic church at the northeast corner of Streetsboro and East Main. The building is now home to Temple Beth Shalom, which conducts Friday evening service twice a month, and the Spiritual Life Society, which conducts Sunday services from September to May. A fenced playground occupies the building's shady side yard along East Main.

Two stained glass windows on the building's south side caught Chuck's eye. He sketched the summery view of the one that was bathed in sunlight. The other had an autumnal look because of the trees growing next to it. One tree was nearly bare of leaves and those remaining were bright red. The other, an evergreen, was covered with Christmas lights.

We crossed the green to read an inscription on a plaque affixed to a rock near the sidewalk on Main Street. It marks the site of a log school, the first in Summit County, built in 1801. The school was used as a meeting place for the First Congregational Church, which was formed in 1802 by David Hudson. The church was the first in Summit and the second in the Western Reserve.

Across Main Street—which is State Route 91, and known as Darrow Road north and south of Hudson—we enjoyed a blueberry phosphate, a soft drink neither of us had heard of before, at Saywell Drug's soda fountain. Then we took a back alley tour of the shops along Main, beginning at the north end, along Owen Brown Street, which is named for the early settler who operated a tannery in town. Owen Brown was also the father of abolitionist John Brown, who was born in Hudson in 1800.

We wound up at the Baldwin-Buss-Merino House at the back end of the park on the northwest corner of Main and Streetsboro. It belongs to Richard Merino, who owns the beverage store next door to the north and the brick building housing Prestige Homes on Streetsboro to the south. The dwelling, built in 1835, is the third oldest home in Hudson, Merino said. His father, the late Gaetano "Charles" Merino, a railroad worker, bought it and some adjacent property in 1907. The father operated a pool hall on the Prestige Homes site and opened the beverage store in what had been his chicken coop, the son said. Richard Merino was one of twelve children and a Hudson High School classmate of former Cleveland Browns great Dante Lavelli and (the late) *Beacon Journal* reporter Frances B. Murphey.

We moved across Streetsboro for a closer look at a log cabin I had long admired from afar. A marker informed us that Boy Scout Troop 321 built it in 1931. The cabin has seen better days and appears to be home to various critters. An elm leaf fashioned from metal is tacked to its rude wooden door. A flagpole between the cabin and a World War I memorial is so overgrown with tree limbs that it is obvious no flag has been raised along the staff in years.

Our last stop was the Hudson Library and Historical Society at 22 Aurora Street. The library annex is dedicated to Caroline Baldwin Babcock, who lived from 1841 to 1921 and founded the library. She also provided funds for a lecture series that bears her name, and Chuck and I were to speak that evening as part of that series. We had dinner with librarian Ron Antonucci and library board member Dorothy Better before facing a friendly audience.

APRIL 7, 1996

The Unseen Peninsula

Songbirds and brilliant sunlight told us it was spring. Easter was just around the corner. The calendar confirmed both of these facts. But the thermometer had been taking us on a roller-coaster ride for days when we went in search of the Peninsula most people never see, walking these short, mostly dead-end streets that run north and south off Main Street—also known as State Route 303. We visited a few days after an early spring snowfall. The snow was gone by the time we got there, having melted less than a day after it had fallen, but the air was still cold enough for us to wear gloves while taking notes. Flotsam on the Cuyahoga River—mostly tree limbs piled beneath the Main Street bridge—wore a fringe of ice that stopped an inch or so above the water.

We had been drawn to Peninsula by the diamond-shaped "No Outlet" signs at the entrances to many of the streets. These streets are home to the people who endure the weekend invasions of tourists and Ohio & Erie Canal towpath hikers and bikers. This was the Peninsula we were looking for. We concentrated on the area west of the bridge, beginning with Canal Street, which parallels the towpath and the river for short distances north and south of Main.

An old building at the southeast corner of Main and South Canal houses the offices of the Cuyahoga Valley Scenic Railroad. From its tiny backyard, we could look down on the towpath, where a short time earlier Chuck had encountered a class on a field trip from Akron's Voris Elementary School. The building, which appears to have once been a private residence, has a garage whose foundation is built into the hillside that runs down to the towpath and the river's edge. It is quite picturesque when seen from below.

North Canal is, for all practical purposes, a private drive that ends where the river bends sharply to the west. A sign in the backyard of the home at the northeast corner of Main and North Canal reads "Dogsled Crossing." Nearby, we saw two dogs and, in a shed, a dogsled.

South Center Street was our next stop. It was here that, in January, we had seen a group of Amish workers building the framework for a garage. We had thought it belonged to one of the houses on Center, but now that it was complete we could tell it went with a home on the next block, Church Street. A lawn sign identifies a rambling two-story Victorian structure on South Center as Centennial House, built in 1876. It is painted tan with trim of teal and brick red, and has an L-shaped porch across the front and one side, plus three smaller porches that are visible from the street.

A tree cast long shadows on the rear of Peninsula's Bronson Memorial Church.

Halfway down the block, we rediscovered a ravine that had been snow-covered on our first visit. This time, it had that springtime look of nature about to burst back into life. Though the evergreens contained the only color to speak of, even the bare trees had that lacy aura that precedes the budding of leaves. Completing the effect were the clusters of snowdrops, tiny white blossoms growing around a low-cut tree stump at the start of the ravine. In January, it had been easy to spot the cardinals against the snowy background. Now we heard more birds than we saw. We admired the remnants of last summer's garden at a home near the end of South Center and then made our way to Church Street, which runs only south of Main—and not very far south at that.

The Bronson Church, a Peninsula landmark, stands at the southeast corner. Its Christmas decorations, pine boughs and red ribbons, had still been up on our first visit. Now the only sign of recent use was birdseed on the front steps and walkway, where a bride and groom had been showered by well-wishers after their wedding. The church was built as Bethel Episcopal in 1839 by the family of Herman Bronson, one of Peninsula's first settlers, who platted the town, according to librarian and historian Randy Bergdorf of the Peninsula Library and Historical Society. Bronson also built the stone house bearing his name on the north side of Main, facing the church. The church was renamed the Bronson Memorial Church in the 1880s and has been owned by the Summit County Historical Society since the mid-1960s.

We walked down Church Street to see the front of that Amish-built garage—and discovered an illustration begging to be drawn: the pale yellow church bathed in sunlight and shadows from a large tree growing in the backyard.

Our only disappointment on our visit was the absence of deer tracks. In January, we found a virtual deer highway—more tracks than either of us had ever seen before—running across wide expanses of snow-covered lawn on both sides of Main, just east of Church Street. Our springtime visit turned up not even one track in the mud.

NOVEMBER 4, 1990

A Foggy Morning in Rogues' Hollow

Was it our imaginations or did the morning fog seem to cling longer to the hills and trees in Rogues' Hollow than elsewhere on the roads to and from the legendary district south of Doylestown? The fog was thick—almost too thick for our purposes—at the start of our visit. But the sun began to burn it off by the time we left Akron with Chuck's wife, Lisa, as our guide. She and friends had gone there as Manchester High School seniors in search of excitement after years of hearing tales about ghosts and witches patrolling the Hollow—and had come home with a few brochures.

Rogues' Hollow is in Wayne County's Chippewa Township, west and slightly north of Clinton and, as mentioned, south of Doylestown. We got there by way of Clinton's Hickory Street, which becomes Galehouse Road after it crosses the Summit-Wayne line. If the district has a boundary, it would seem to be defined by Galehouse, Hametown, Clinton, and Rogue Hollow Roads. (Road signs and maps do not use a possessive with the word "Rogue.")

Rogues' Hollow got its name from the hard-drinking, roughneck coal miners who populated the region from the late 1820s, after the Ohio & Erie Canal opened, until late in the nineteenth century. By the 1860s and 1870s, miners' brawling and menacing of travelers earned the Hollow the reputation as "the toughest damn spot in the United States," according to published accounts. The late Al Capp might have been inspired by Rogues' Hollow when he created Dogpatch, the backwoods environment for his cartoon character, Li'l Abner. The Hollow bears a striking resemblance to remote spots in Kentucky.

We circumnavigated the area by car, looking for but never finding "the witch's house" (the Manchester High students' name for a home where a resident sold Rogues' Hollow brochures in the 1970s). We parked in a clearing along Galehouse across from an unpainted, ancient-looking mill on Silver Creek. Before we stopped, we saw fields filled with rows of the summer's cornstalks, road signs so covered with vines that the names could not be read, a "No Dumping" sign riddled with bullet holes, and a family of turtles sunning on rocks in a stream.

A few paces east of the mill we crossed over Cry-Baby Bridge, where, according to legend, at midnight one can hear the cries of a baby who was tossed into the creek many years ago. Standing there on a foggy autumn morning, the only sounds we heard were the water flowing below, the crunching of leaves underfoot, and the buzzing of the pesky mosquitoes whose environment we had invaded. Traffic across the bridge has worn grooves through the asphalt and into the deck's wooden planking, but it was otherwise quite ordinary looking.

At the edge of the road in front of the mill was a large wooden Rogues' Hollow Historical Society sign. A "Closed" sign hung in one of the mill's seven front windows and no hours were posted, so we had to be content with an exterior exploration of the grounds. A thick old sycamore stood just east of the mill. Two main branches reached out and then upward, reminding us of the Signal Tree at the Chuckery in the Cascade Valley park north of Akron. Two young evergreens flanked a sandstone walkway leading from the road to the heavy plank front door of the mill. A fire circle held what looked like the remnants of a corn roast, and a gas grill and lawn chairs suggested recent occupancy of the place. We learned later that the mill just looked old. It is a 1976 replica of the nineteenth-century woolen mill operated on the site by Albert and Sarah Chidester. The wooden water wheel, according to a plaque on the building, was built by the late Joe Overholt in memory of his mother, Maggie Smith Overholt, who worked at the mill in her youth.

In the weeds alongside the mill, we found an old grinding stone and, on a short section of rusty track, a four-wheeled wooden coal car from some long-forgotten mine. Out back, we followed a path through the brush until the mosquitoes scared us off. But that's as scared as we got during our hourlong visit. We heard or saw no signs of the ghosts of Peg Leg Pete, the one-legged wagon driver, or Big Mike Walsh, the three-hundred-pound saloonkeeper, to mention two of the Hollow's legendary figures. In fact, we saw no one at all. It was eerie, especially before the fog lifted, but not scary.

Fog covered the Cry-Baby Bridge in Rogues' Hollow.

Halfway up Galehouse hill, severe water runoff has exposed the roots of many trees along the road. One had roots the thickness of a man's thigh reaching in every direction and forming a shelter large enough for a person to curl up in. The terrain flattens out at the top of the hill, and the road forks. Galehouse takes a sharp turn to the left, leading travelers through a section of homes built within the last fifteen or twenty years. Straight ahead begins Rogue Hollow Road. A tall four-sided wooden post identifies the roads in white letters against a black background.

My late *Beacon Journal* colleague Bill Bierman wrote in 1976 that the Hollow's mystique is so persistent that new tales are still being "invented." He credited the power of suggestion reinforced by a "good buzz on." I wish we could add to the lore, but we were cold sober on the day of our visit. Perhaps we should return some moonlit night.

Not on your life.

SEPTEMBER 6, 1987

Strolling through a Small Town

It isn't Lake Wobegon or Mayberry, but Doylestown certainly is the type of place that inspired these fictional American small towns. As in Garrison Keillor's mythical Minnesota hometown, Catholics and Lutherans have been worshiping side by side in churches that have seen several seasons of weathering and repair. And like the setting for Andy Griffith's television sitcom of the 1960s, Doylestown has a flagpole in the middle of its downtown intersection.

But Doylestown goes Mayberry one better. Standing at attention beneath the Stars and Stripes and the MIA banner at Portage and Clinton Streets is a bronze doughboy, a reminder that, for the eighty-eight boys who "answered the call of their country" in World War I, life was no sitcom. Motorists are cautioned to keep right at the often-busy intersection. And strollers wanting a closer look at the inscription on the war memorial draw stares.

All four corners of the intersection invite closer inspection. The north-west corner, ablaze with colorful flowers all summer, was landscaped in memory of departed residents Doris Smith, Gladys Dayton, and Helen Pamer. Diagonally across the intersection is the forty-six-year-old band terrace, its masonry design testimony to the time in which it was built. Standing like large bookends on the other corners, twin cannons point skyward.

At 160, Doylestown is old enough to have replaced most of its oldest structures with buildings that are now themselves old. Its thirteen-year-old village hall, on Clinton at Portage, replaced a ninety-six-year-old relic that once was an opera house. Originally, the site was occupied by the Billman House Hotel, which thrived in the village's days as a stagecoach stop on the Cleveland-Akron-Wooster route.

The arched entrance to Jake's pizza shop on the east side of Portage, in a two-story red-brick structure built to house the Doylestown Banking Company, provides a shady vantage point for people-watching on a hot day. A sign out front marks the spot as the site of village founder William Doyle's tavern. Fittingly, the building is flanked by bars from which the aroma of beer wafts.

Across the street, Paridon's Hardware occupies half of the ground floor of the 101-year-old Odd Fellows building. The late Anthony "Andy" Paridon moved the business there in 1939 after operating on the square for thirteen years, according to his son, Frank. Another son, Leo, and his wife, Twila, are the owners. Another second-generation business on Portage is the eighty-eight-year-old Doylestown Telephone Company, founded by the late E.W. Stepfield and now run by his son, Donald.

And down the street, Ira Lepley pumps gas and works on cars at the gas station started in 1924 by his grandfather, Charles. The owner is his uncle, Harry Lepley, who runs an antique shop next door.

Doylestown's ties to Akron are many. Akron physician Eliakun Crosby is credited with naming Rogues' Hollow, just south of the village. He built cabins there for the workers in the coal mines that flourished along Silver Creek from around 1840 until 1887. Saints Peter and Paul Catholic Church, established in 1827, sent a mission team to Akron in 1837 to establish its first

*Zion Lutheran Church dates to 1867, the
year Doylestown was incorporated.*

Catholic parish, St. Vincent's. On the other side of a hedgerow, a modern entrance blends nicely with much-older brickwork at Zion Lutheran Church, where the cornerstone reads 1867, the year the village was incorporated.

Standing on the tree-covered lawn that separates Doylestown's Lutherans and Catholics, it isn't hard to imagine a visitor finding the same sense of serenity here one hundred years from now.

NOVEMBER 5, 1989

Treading Water

Water Street in Kent is many things to many people. To visitors coming via Interstate 76, it is State Route 43, a country road that suddenly becomes urban, leading to City Hall and the downtown area. It is a place to shop, fill the gas tank, have a bite to eat, or check into a motel. And Water Street is a residential neighborhood, although that came as a surprise when we walked the five blocks between Bowman and Summit Streets. Sure, we knew that Kent is a city of some 26,000 residents and nearly 24,000 Kent campus students. Chuck is a Kent State University graduate, and I have often visited the city and campus. But we were seeing the homes for the first time as we walked along the sidewalks on both sides of Water Street on a warm fall day.

We hadn't planned to walk along Water. Our goal was to share impressions of the campus in autumn—after lunch at one of the many eateries whose signs beckoned as we drove into town. We changed our plans in the pizza parlor as we saw the street from a different perspective. Across the parking lot was an old white house. Behind it on the same lot was another, neat as a pin, with a garage that seemed to be losing its battle with gravity. An orange pickup truck was parked in the yard. To at least two families, we decided, Water Street was more than an avenue to and from other places. It was home.

Our walk started and ended on Water, as our pedestrian perspective revealed a treelined street of wonderful old homes that had previously been hidden by our inability or unwillingness to see them when we hurried about in cars. We saw front porches, side porches, and wraparound porches on houses of all sizes, colors, shapes, and conditions, many with slate roofs and gingerbread trim. The dwellings ranged from one wearing fake red brick and a ragged green shade on a front window to one right out of *Better Homes and Gardens.*

The showplace was a small two-story, gray, shake-shingled home with a white-spindled railing on a wraparound porch, which had a two-seater swing hanging from its ceiling. Flowerbeds were bordered with perfectly placed rocks. The Stars and Stripes waved in the breeze. The other caught our eye not because of the fake brick siding that was popular in the 1920s and 1930s, but because of the five-foot-tall weeds that grew in the driveway in front of the open door of its small one-car garage.

The front lawn at another house was decorated with an untitled sculpture, four sections of barkless log connected to each other by metal strips and hanging between a tree on one end and two poles and an old tire on the other.

The block between Elm and Oak Streets was lined with seven homes that stood on such high ground that concrete stairs had been cut into the front lawns. The stairs and steel banisters all matched, suggesting the work was done at the same time by the same workers, probably when the street was widened some twenty years ago.

On a much larger scale, a concrete retaining wall and stairs with three landings had been added to the front of a green home near the southwest corner of Water and Summit Streets. Tie-dyed curtains and jerry-built entrances and stairways suggested that some of the houses were student rentals.

At Williams and Water Streets, we paused for a close-up look at Trinity Lutheran Church. It is a handsome gray-stone building from any angle, looking much newer than the dates on its cornerstone—1884 and 1908. A worn, barely visible sign reads "First Evangelical Lutheran Church." A newer plaque, presented by the Kent Bicentennial Commission, marks it as a preserved historical site erected in 1884.

The sound of children drew our attention as we neared the corner of School and Water Streets. Pupils at Holden School were being dismissed at the close of the school day. As we prepared to drive away, a black squirrel scampered off while two little girls walked arm in arm to the house with the crooked garage.

MAY 3, 1987

Strolling through Chippewa Lake

It's hard to say which is more spectacular, sunrise or sunset at Chippewa Lake. Phyllis Thibodeaux watches them both from her yard, which ends where the beach begins on the east shore of the 386-acre lake in Medina County's Lafayette and Westfield Townships. Listen to her talk about it: "The farmhouse across the lake looks like it's on fire when the sun starts to rise. And the sunsets. . . . During the summer, no one leaves for home until they've watched the sun set. You just can't describe the view. You have to live it."

Thibodeaux, who grew up in Lafayette, Louisiana, has been living it for three and a half years. She and her son Neil, fifteen, a freshman at Cloverleaf High School, live in one of seven homes that are occupied year-round in the section of Lafayette Township just north of Chippewa Lake Park. The rest are cottages, most of them well maintained, a handful vacant and falling down.

Bruce Biliczky, Thibodeaux's neighbor and landlord, has lived at Chippewa Lake since he was born thirty-six years ago. He learned to swim in the lake and hunts and fishes there. He calls the vacant, rundown cottages in his neighborhood "bombed-out buildings" and has complained to township and county officials about them for years. Many of the cottages are owned by Chippewa Lake Properties Incorporated, a subsidiary of Cleveland-based Continental Business Enterprises Incorporated, which also owns the lake, its beach, and the amusement park, which closed at the end of its one hundredth season in 1978.

We strolled along the eastern shore's sandy beach during the quiet time before the start of the boating and fishing seasons. The only signs of life we saw under a cloudless sky were distant—vapor trails from gleaming dots in the sky, an occasional glimpse of a car zipping along Ballash Road on the west shore, and, of course, the gulls. Beached not far from the park's bathhouse is an old excursion boat, its name, *Show Boat,* all but faded from its rusting hull.

Up the hill is the midway, looking like something out of Stephen King's imagination. Weeds, some as tall as seven feet, grow through the blacktop. Where once there were thirty rides, traces of only three remain—the skeleton of the wooden roller coaster, the cars and track of "the Bug," and a rusted Ferris wheel frame. With part of the "R" missing, the sign on one building reads "APCADE." But the sixty-four-year-old ballroom, closed since 1971 except for brief usage for rock performances in 1977, a restaurant, "The Original Hamburger Factory," and the old hotel look as if they're just a few coats of paint away from being used. That's not likely, says G. E. DiGeronimo, head of Continental Business Enterprises. The park has been for sale since before its final season. "There are two or three leads, but there's nothing to talk about."

It is the park that most people remember when Chippewa Lake is mentioned. But the lake was the initial attraction. The Chippewa Indians hunted and fished there before the first white hunters and trappers moved into the area after the War of 1812. Westfield Township was organized in 1820. Lafayette Township, originally part of Westfield, was incorporated twelve years later. The village of Chippewa-on-the-Lake, consisting of sixteen lake-front lots, was incorporated in 1873. With a population of less than 250 today, it is the smallest of three villages that occupy the lake's east shore. The others are Briarwood Beach, which incorporated in 1956 and today has more than six hundred residents, and Gloria Glens, a fifty-four-year-old community with a population exceeding four hundred.

Rumors about the sale of the park and the lake circulate "constantly," according to Jean Jackson, a twelve-year Gloria Glens resident. "Everyone is afraid of seeing the whole area built up with apartments or townhouses, but everyone wants something done about the park," she said.

Homes across the lake were visible through the midway at Chippewa Lake Park.

Bill Parker, twenty-nine, owner of the Chippewa Lake Café in Briarwood Beach and a Gloria Glens resident, lamented the fact that nothing is being done with the park. "I can't believe that the person who owns it would let it just sit there and rot," said Parker, who grew up in Hinckley and often went to the park in his youth. He said he settled in Gloria Glens because "you don't have to worry about your kids around here" and because the setting was reminiscent of the area around Conneaut Lake in northwestern Pennsylvania where his wife Kathleen grew up.

DiGeronimo allows residents to use the beaches and the lake. Chippewa-on-the-Lake residents and those in the section of the township adjacent to the lake have free access. Gloria Glens and Briarwood Beach residents pay annual fees that vary according to how long they've owned their property. This is a modification of the arrangement residents had enjoyed for years with Parker Beach, who rescued the park from bankruptcy in 1937 and ran it for thirty-three years before selling the lake, park, and an additional forty-five acres to DiGeronimo in 1970. Beach had worked at the park as a boy when his father, Albert McDowell Beach, was manager and later owner. Cleveland businessman Edwin L. Andrews developed the park as a summer resort in the 1870s. The elder Beach, who began leasing the park in 1878, installed the first rides around the turn of the century.

The early years have been chronicled in interviews and more than two hundred photographs by Sharon Kraynek in her book, *Chippewa Lake Park, 1800–1978, Diary of an Amusement Park* (Apollo, Pennsylvania: Closson Press, 1987). Kraynek, a Pittsburgh teacher who lives at the lake every summer, spent eight years doing her research. The book is an attempt to keep alive the memories of the park.

"I hated to see what happened to it," said Kraynek, who grew up in Lakewood. "There's a whole generation that's missed it. I went back to when the Indians were there to the time the park closed. I interviewed people in their nineties. They were so frail, so delicate. It's as if they were reliving their lives." Kraynek, her husband John, and their three children usually leave for Chippewa "the day school lets out," she said. "Years ago, my family had a cottage on

Shady Slope Drive. We bought three cottages. We keep two for ourselves and one to rent. As dilapidated as it [the park] is, people want to be there."

They want to be there in summer, when as many as forty sailboats skim the waters. They want to watch teenagers dancing with grandmothers at autumn clambakes. They want to skate on the winter ice or fish through holes cut in it. And they want to hear the tingle, like wind chimes, as the ice breaks up in the spring.

JULY 7, 1991

Looking beyond the Obvious

You really can't judge a book by its cover or the interior of a building by its facade. Come with us to Canton to learn, as we did, about just three of its old gems. We had a guide on a six-block stroll that embraced some of the city's oldest and newest structures. *Beacon Journal* correspondent Betty O'Neill-Roderick was eager to show us her hometown's historic district. We certainly would have found the Saxton House on our own, but we might have over-looked the Canton Classic Car Museum without our guide's direction. And there's no doubt we would never have seen the old Barber-Whitticar House had she not pointed it out.

The Canton Hilton, until recently called the Newmarket Hilton, was our starting point. The Hilton, the garage, and the United Bank were built five years ago in the Newmarket renewal project, which replaced an older generation of buildings that included the McKinley Hotel, O'Neill-Roderick reported. The three structures are linked in architectural design and by skywalks that make it possible to go from one to the others without venturing out into the elements.

We ventured across Market to see the Canton Rotary Newmarket Park, created in 1986 by the Rotary Club with help from the Stark County Foundation, Metro Ceramics, the students at Timken High School, and Motter Meadows, architects. The brick pavement bears names of park benefactors or

Canton's Saxton House, now the home of the First Ladies Museum, was where Ida Saxton and future President William McKinley had their wedding reception in 1871.

deceased family members in whose names many of the bricks were purchased.

While O'Neill-Roderick and I counted bricks, Chuck found the subject of his illustration, the Saxton House, which stands just south of the park at 331 Market Avenue South. Instead of choosing the view most popular with photographers, the front of the house, with its wraparound porch and mill-wheel marker, the artist found a vantage point in the parking lot at the rear, which captured the old building in a context with its Newmarket neighbors. That the Saxton House stands at all is a testimony to its sound construction and the recent commitment of Canton residents to historic preservation. It was built by James A. Saxton, founder of the *Ohio Repository* and father of Ida Saxton, the wife of President William McKinley. The home was about six years old when the McKinleys were married in 1871. Their wedding reception was held in the grand ballroom on the third floor.

M. J. Albacete, director of the Canton Art Institute, described the brick structure as "a Second Empire house of simple nobility," in the book *Architecture in Canton: 1805–1976*, published in 1976 by the institute and the Junior League of Canton. In the years after the Saxtons and McKinleys departed the premises, the house was used for a variety of businesses. An addition was built on the front for retail space and, as photographs indicate, the structure bore little resemblance to its original grandeur.

Exterior renovation supported by the preservation society is essentially complete, but the interior is a work in progress. Last year, the home was leased to Drs. Jan and Richard Schwartz for a unique antique business, Leon Richard Antiquaires. Jan is a psychologist and Richard is a physician. Their business is nonprofit, with all proceeds earmarked for the Canton Redevelopment Fund. Old beams and wall lath (the framework for wall plaster in the era before drywall) remain exposed in the first-floor gallery, and a ribbon and an "under construction" sign at the foot of a grand stairway warn visitors not to venture upstairs. Because the home is listed on the National Register of Historic Places, the Schwartzes have had to get specific permission for virtually everything they've done since the business opened; they cannot alter the physical structure in any way.

Our next stop was Created for You, an art gallery and shop selling gourmet coffees, pastries, ice cream, and sandwiches in a turreted Victorian home at 519 Cleveland Avenue South. The proprietors, Jan and Tom Murphy, said they bought the eighty-seven-year-old relic three and a half years ago after discovering they couldn't buy the Saxton House. It is known as the Barber-Whitticar House because it was built in 1904 by Orrin Barber, Ida Saxton McKinley's nephew, and went on to become the Whitticar funeral home from 1920 to 1974. Unlike the Saxton House, the Barber-Whitticar House is utilized from stem to stern. The Murphys live upstairs. Jan Murphy teaches oil painting and creates her own artwork in a studio at the rear. Her husband, aided by a small staff, operates the kitchen and dining rooms. A bonus feature of the place, Tom Murphy said, is the front porch, from which the owners and their guests have the best view in town of the Pro Football Hall of Fame parade. The Murphys' restoration is having a positive effect on the neighborhood, Tom said. "We paint a board, our neighbors paint a board."

Our last stop was the Canton Classic Car Museum, Marshall Belden's private collection of thirty beauties at 555 Market Avenue South. Curator Don Prince let us browse on our own, then offered a bit of history. The museum opened eleven years ago in what had been an auto-repair garage.

APRIL 9, 2000

Paris in the Springtime

If this page were a musical score, the title at the top might well be "April in Paris." If this were a postcard, there wouldn't be enough room to tell the story of our visit to Paris, a tiny crossroads community in southeastern Stark County.

Neither of us had ever heard of Paris, Ohio, until Chuck found a reproduction copy of the 1875 Stark County atlas at the McKinley Museum in

Canton. (He bought two copies, one of which he gave me as a retirement gift.) Leafing through the atlas, Chuck spotted a map of Paris Township. Minerva is at its southeast corner, but it was the village of Paris near the northwest corner that caught his eye. A trip to Paris in the springtime was inevitable. All I had to do was study up on the subject and pack a notebook and my new camera (a retirement gift from my family).

Paris's history is summed up on page twenty-two of the atlas, and, by coincidence, this story is an anniversary piece of sorts. The township was incorporated on April 1, 1818, and its first election was held April 11—in Paris. The larger town of Minerva, "laid out in the winter of 1833–34," dominates the history, which was written 125 years ago, but Jacob Gerwig's large orchard on the outskirts of Paris is singled out for mention.

The 1875 map on page 113 shows two hotels and two stores at Main Street (today's Lisbon Road and State Route 172) and Pekin Road (now called Paris Road). A Methodist Episcopal church sits just south of Main near the intersection, and a doctor's office is across the street. Gerwig's property dominates the map's southwestern corner. A school on Pekin backs up to it, and the Lutheran and German Reformed Church is shown on the town's largest single parcel across the street. Other identified properties include a tannery at the north end of town, a barbershop, a shoe store, and two parcels marked "Furn St.," which we guess might mean "furniture store."

We found the road to Paris on Chuck's contemporary map. Its northern terminus is on Alberta Beach Road, just east of State Route 44. We found Alberta Beach, a hilly two-lane thoroughfare with no difficulty, and knew we were in for a treat when we spotted the yellow bend-in-the-road sign with the word "Paris" beneath the big black arrow. Chuck stopped to get a photo of the sign, and I grabbed a shot of him taking his picture.

The road to Paris defines the term "middle of nowhere." It's bumpy and, as we headed south, began to resemble someone's driveway. Just as we wondered if we had taken a wrong turn, we came to an intersection where the pavement improved again, and in a few minutes found ourselves staring at the Paris Community Pavilion at the southwest corner of Lisbon and Paris.

The pavilion, which bears the Lions Club insignia, stands in a small grassy park decorated with the Stars and Stripes and a cannon in honor of all who served their country in the military. A red-painted cast-iron water pump completes the town square picture. There was so much to see, we didn't know where to start. Just west of the park was a scene reminiscent of Colonial Williamsburg, a row of buildings faced in brick or shake shingles or both.

Across from the pavilion, at the northwest corner of the intersection, stood an apparently vacant two-story frame structure that became the focus of today's illustration. Covered with peeling blue and white paint, it looked like an old country inn that had seen better days. It was wide and twice as long, suggesting that one of the hotels listed on the 1875 map might have been there. The sidewalk out front was paved with red bricks, and a porch stretched across one third of the building's long west side. Display windows across half the front suggested it might have been the store listed on the old map. Chuck decided to show downtown Paris through these windows.

We found the large church parcel just south of the intersection. Israel's Evangelical Lutheran Church dates to at least 1848, according to the cornerstone, and occupies a building erected in 1927. The rest of the parcel is its cemetery, which surrounds the church on three sides and affords a breathtaking view of the hilly rural landscape for miles to the east and south.

On the way back to Lisbon and Paris, we stopped at the Paris Community Building, which, according to a stone marker on its front, was the Embry Chapel of the Methodist Episcopal Church, built in 1873—just in time to be included in the old atlas.

Our last stop was the Paris post office, a tiny one-story brick structure built in 1964–65 on the foundation of an older post office, according to Keith Best, postmaster since 1993. The address is 12550 Lisbon Road, and the zip code is 44669. Best estimated that one hundred to one hundred and fifty people live in Paris and said there are five hundred in his delivery area. He said he gets a lot of errant mail intended for delivery in Portage County's Paris Township, which is served by the Newton Falls post office.

The postmaster invited us back for the Memorial Day parade, which, he said, attracts people from miles around. Signs for a parade-planning meeting were hung at the post office and elsewhere in town. Sunrises are spectacular in Paris, Best said. In fact, he said, *Sunrise in Paris* was the title of an art exhibit at Mount Union College in Alliance. The late Fran Murphey would have been disappointed to learn that we left without mailing a postcard from Paris. But, borrowing a page from her book, we both came away with scores of pictures quite suitable for use as postcards.

Epilogue

Nothing lasts forever, but for a while it seemed our *Akron Beacon Journal* series about the simple pleasures of walking just might be immune to the vagaries of the newspaper business. The feature survived artist Chuck Ayers' departure from the newspaper in 1994 to concentrate on his work on the syndicated comic strips *Crankshaft* and *Funky Winkerbean.* It continued running in the *Beacon* magazine, with Chuck contributing on a freelance basis, until the magazine folded in 1995.

But that wasn't the end. Our walks were featured in the newspaper for the next five years and returned to the magazine when its publication resumed in 2000. It took the second demise of the magazine to end our *Beacon Journal* run in December of that year.

Our twenty-first century wish list included walking over Akron—literally—if we could hitch a ride on the Goodyear blimp. We never got to write that story for the *Beacon Journal,* but there's nothing stopping us from doing it now. True, I've never been up in the blimp, but Chuck has—twice—and he was delighted to share his overview of Akron for this book. Seeing his hometown from the gondola of the Goodyear blimp was a dream come true, Chuck said, and getting two rides was more than twice the pleasure.

My lasting impression of being over downtown Akron was the opposite of what I imagined it would be. I always thought of Akron having a lot of buildings and no place to park. You still hear people say that parking is at such a premium downtown. In reality, downtown Akron has lots of parking and very few buildings. I was quite surprised as we flew over downtown to see all these empty parking lots. They surrounded almost every building. There were so many more parking places than there were buildings. And there are fewer buildings now than there were then.

Both times Chuck went up, in 1979 and 1982, the passengers were members of the news media and their family members or other guests.

They were sending up a lot of people, six at a time. Every half hour, they'd take off from the Akron Municipal Airport, and thirty minutes later they'd come back and be on the ground just long enough to unload those six people and get six more people onboard. We flew northeast from the airport. We crossed downtown moving in a northerly direction, pretty much paralleling Main Street. We were a bit east of downtown, so our view was sort of looking to the west as we proceeded north.

The scale is what surprised me. I remembered the major parts of Main Street being sort of canyonlike when seen from the ground. Akron isn't New York City or even Cleveland, but you're pretty much boxed in on Main Street. Even as broad as Main Street is, the only sky you saw was directly overhead. But looking down from the gondola, everything looked so compact to the ground. The First Merit Tower and the larger buildings at Cascade Plaza really stood out.

I had seen downtown from the air flying back from vacations. That same feeling hit me. You see the buildings. But you see so many more trees. You're much more aware of the trees from the air than you are from the ground. Akron isn't a huge city, but you tend to think of it as bigger. A big part of what a blimp ride does for you is that you sense that scale. And the fact that the blimp moves so slowly—the top speed is thirty-five to forty miles an hour—correlates to our walks around town because we moved so leisurely.

Another lasting impression: As soon as the blimp gains any altitude at all, you're above the level of all the downtown buildings, and while you're still over the airport, you can see downtown Akron, and, thirty-five miles beyond it, the skyline of Cleveland. Coming from the south, in my field of view, there were times when I was looking at both cities at the same time.

Chuck's second blimp ride provided some thrills and chills because of high winds.

The Central Interchange was the farthest away from the airport we could get. We flew into the wind for about twenty-five minutes, then in five minutes—*Phmph!*—we were back at the airport.

What's it like to ride on a windy day, when the blimp rocks back and forth?

I don't know any of the physics involved, and I don't know exactly how it works, but it's not like sitting in a swing, going back and forth. It's more like sitting at the fulcrum of a teeter-totter. It's more like being on a rocking chair. It's like the bag is rotating over the weight of the gondola, and so it's much smoother than it looks. It's very smooth and very comfortable.

But it's also quite noisy as the blimp's engines are working hard. The noise caused the young daughter of one passenger to cry. The pilot came to the rescue, asking what the problem was.

"Too noisy," the girl's father said.

"We can handle that," the pilot replied, turning off the engines.

The propellers were still freewheeling, making a whistling sound, but the roar of the engines stopped. "I don't know about everybody else, but my first instinct was to grab my chair and think 'we are going down!' But we didn't. We just sat there. To be in the air and backing up was the strangest experience. We couldn't get up very high because of the wind. But it was just so neat to see the ground going by as we were moving backwards. We did this for several minutes, five or less. But what an experience. And then the pilot started up the engines again, and we turned and, going with the wind, went right down into the airport."

Now that, dear readers, is what I call an overview.

Index